THE TESTIMONY BOOK

THIRTY-ONE STORIES FROM AROUND THE WORLD

THE TESTIMONY BOOK

THIRTY-ONE STORIES FROM AROUND THE WORLD

EDITED & COMPILED BY
BEN BLOCK

THE TESTIMONY BOOK

Published by KDP

Feel free to share the stories and the contents of this book.

ISBN 979-8-9872967-1-4 (paperback)
ISBN 979-8-9872967-0-7 (ebook)

Translation of Junko Mouri's testimony: Christine Huber, Google Translate, & DeepL Translator
Translation of Mirian Almeida's testimony: Paul & Priscilla Hrubik and Google Translate

Formatting: Jen Henderson
Cover Design: Rick Lundskow
Editor: Ben Block

Visit the editor's website at theblockfam.com.

All proceeds from the sales of *The Testimony Book* will go to Paz International to aid in planting churches and making disciples of Jesus.

PSALM 96:3 (NLT)

Publish his glorious deeds among the nations.
Tell everyone about the amazing things he does.

ENDORSEMENTS FOR THE TESTIMONY BOOK

"Having personally experienced emotional trauma, divine healing, powerful encounters with God and the challenges of 40 years as a missionary, I could identify with all of the testimonies in Ben's book. I could feel the pain and rejoice with each person sharing their struggles and victories. Their stories will boost your faith to believe God for the touch you need from Him in whatever situation you are facing! We serve an awesome God and He wants to meet you in a personal way just as he did each one in this book!"

JEFF HRUBIK
President, Paz International, Santarém, Brazil

"Benjamin Block shares a collection of modern-day miracle stories that demonstrate the power and extravagant love of God. *The Testimony Book* will inspire confidence and propel you in your walk with God, knowing that God still works mightily today in and through the lives of ordinary people."

JAMIE VAN VLIET
Top-producing Real Estate Team, Michael Saunders & Co, Sarasota, FL

"We are familiar with stories in our world that are tragic, painful and hold a great amount of despair. They come at us from all angles; social media, news outlets and even those we know and love. While it's important to walk in empathy, compassion and love toward these things, our culture often elevates the bad over the good. We can't ignore the reality that the powerful hand of God is moving all the time! People are facing difficult moments in life, while finding hope, peace, joy and supernatural grace in the person of Jesus Christ. This book elevates those stories so we can remember the good is conquering the bad. Life is more powerful than death. Light is breaking through the darkness in real people's lives!"

AMREITHA JEEVA
Co-Lead Pastor, Kalos Church, Seattle, WA

"Ben Block is an incredible author and an even greater man of God and I am so excited for his new book! I believe it will bless you, it will encourage you, it will challenge you, and it will grow you to be who God's called you to be. I am so excited for the words and the impact that this book will have on the next generation and every person who reads it. I also believe that this book of testimonies will be a book that inspires people to trust God through every season of life and pursue the God-given dreams and callings that are on their lives. And I believe Ben's words of what other people have walked through and faced in their own life will help breathe fresh hope and victory in your life."

PAUL DAUGHERTY
Co-Lead Pastor, Victory Church, Tulsa, OK

*To **Debbie**, the woman in the world who I love and enjoy the most, who can light up a room and my life with her smile, and who I look forward to living for Jesus with for the rest of my life.*

*To my beautiful daughters, **Isabella**, **Evelyn**, and **Eliana**. I love you so much, girls. Let's always live for Jesus. We have a wonderful life and eternity in front of us! And to my fourth daughter, **Esther Joelle**, who is in heaven. Can't wait to spend time with you in eternity with Jesus!*

*To the **God of miracles**. Thank You so much for being actively a part of our lives every day.*

CONTENTS

SALVATION STORIES

ENCOUNTERS WITH GOD

MIRACLES

PHYSICAL HEALINGS

EMOTIONAL HEALINGS

ACKNOWLEDGEMENTS

I first and foremost want to acknowledge God Almighty. He's amazing and He is the reason this book exists. Thank You, Heavenly Father God, for doing all these wonderful and amazing miracles!

I want to thank each person who contributed a story of what God did in your life and allowed me to share it with others. Your stories are amazing! I've enjoyed reading them and I'm excited to share them with the world! May God be glorified!

Thank you, Debbie, for believing in me and supporting me in this journey of making this dream of a book come into reality. Thank you for helping me think through many items pertaining to this book and for all the mini conversations to flesh out ideas. And for listening to me as I gave you updates about how the book is coming along!

Thank you, Jen Henderson, for answering a bunch of questions about writing and creating a book. Thank you for all the Zoom calls and helping me along the way. And thank you for formatting this book!

Thank you, Rick Lundskow, for designing the book cover and using your talents to glorify God. Love you man!

Thank you, Aunt Christine Huber, for reviewing the translation for Junko Mouri's testimony from Japanese to English.

Thank you, Paul and Pri Hrubik, for translating Pastor Mirian Almeida's testimony from Portuguese to English.

INTRODUCTION

CREATING A BOOK FULL OF TESTIMONIES

The idea to create a book full of testimonies came to me about 15 years ago. I was driving on the highway in California on summer break from college and I felt the Lord give me the idea to create this book. I remember pulling over on the side of the road and writing the ideas down.

I thought it would be so easy to make this book and for years I wanted to do it. Turns out it was harder than I thought! But at the beginning of 2021 I felt like the Lord put it on my heart to make it happen. I had planned to do it in the last quarter of the year.

However, in September of 2021 our fourth daughter suddenly died just two weeks before my wife's scheduled delivery date. Needless to say, that took the wind out of my sails.

Thankfully, God is still good. He's still on the throne. He's helped heal our hearts. It's a personal testimony of ours that God helped us get through that season and one that my wife, Debbie, shares about later in this book.

After being postponed about one year, God helped me get the ball rolling. I'm very grateful for each individual who took the time to record their stories of God's miracles in their lives. As I've edited this book, I've tried to keep the original meaning of each testimony.

These stories are incredibly moving. They've made me smile from ear to ear. I am extremely grateful for the things God has done even in my own family's lives as I read some of their testimonies.

This book contains the miracles of God in different people's lives from people all over the world—literally, from four different continents.

There are 31 testimonies included. You can read them one at a time over the course of a month or you can binge read them all at once!

The Bible says in Psalm 77:14 (NIV) "You are the God who performs miracles; you display your power among the peoples." Our God is the One True God who does miracles and displays His power among us.

As you read, I pray your faith is encouraged. I hope you are inspired to believe God to do a miracle in your own life! He is the God who heals, who delivers, who saves, who reconciles, and who does the impossible.

He has done miracles all throughout history and He's still doing them today. He is the God of miracles, and these are just a few of the testimonies!

SALVATION STORIES

1.
THE FAITH I ONCE MOCKED I SOON JOINED

BY MEGAN LIBKUMAN
MICHIGAN, USA

---

*"I am the good shepherd.
The good shepherd lays down
his life for the sheep."*

—JOHN 10:11 (NIV)

Growing up I went to church on holidays but I only understood it to be about rituals and repetition. Through attending those few church services over the years as a child I never knew the gospel or that Jesus died for my sins or even that I was a sinner at all. I didn't even realize that Jesus wasn't just an ominous statue on a stained-glass wall of a man with thorns around His head.

If I had understood Who Jesus is, what He had done for me, and that trusting and believing in Him would allow me to be with Him in eternity forever, I may not have had a deep fear of death as a child—one that would cause endless stomachaches and upset in the dark hours of night. It was a fear that my parents, not knowing Jesus themselves, had no tools or words of comfort and peace to give me to calm the fears.

If I had known, as a teen, of my Heavenly Father who loved me so much that He would send His only begotten Son to save me from my sins I would've known to run from those sins rather than falling into every trap the enemy would throw at me: lying, stealing, addiction, promiscuity, dishonor to my parents—and more than anything, dishonoring the One who created me in His image.

As an adult, I became bitter toward the church, and didn't understand its purpose! On occasion as I would drive by a church I would mockingly "baaa" toward the building, thinking "church people are sheep," not even knowing the irony that the Bible actually calls the Lord a Shepherd!

However, I was invited to a young adult church service by a friend… and I said yes. There was no Jesus statue on the wall, it was the words of Jesus being preached that gave me life, knowledge, and understanding about the good news of Jesus Christ! I learned that I was a sinner in need of a Savior and there was only one way! I accepted Christ into my life and asked Him for forgiveness and have been walking with Him for about 8 years.

Where I once was without understanding, I now understand my purpose is to glorify God with my life and to reflect His character in everything I say and do. I don't do this perfectly but His Word says He began a good work in me and will not stop working on me every moment that I walk this earth.

Prayer: *Heavenly Father God, please help me know the truth of what Your Son Jesus did for me and give me boldness to share it with others. In Jesus' name I pray, amen.*

2.
DRUNK WITH ALCOHOL TO FILLED WITH THE SPIRIT

BY CURTIS BLOCK
IOWA, USA

"Therefore, if anyone is in Christ, he is a new creation; old things have passed away; behold, all things have become new."

—2 CORINTHIANS 5:17 (NKJV)

I have never shared my testimony this way before but I do hope that it will lift Jesus up and encourage and inspire others and maybe keep some from making the mistakes I've made in my life.

Growing up during the Vietnam Era—make love, not war, question the establishment—drinking was the norm in our family gatherings. At the age of 14 I started drinking and was buying liquor when I was 16. I played in all the sports and activities in high school and college, but drinking was a major social activity. In college, I developed a taste for pot. I loved the smell of it and the feeling and smoked a lot of it.

I started listening to a Christian radio station out of Omaha, Nebraska while I was on the road during the day working. I'd turn it back to a rock and roll station in case somebody got in the car with me that night! Romans 10:17 (NKJV) says that "Faith comes by hearing and hearing by the Word of God." I'd listen to people like Kenneth Hagin, Kenneth Copeland, and R. W. Schambach.

They would be talking about people receiving healing in their bodies by a God that was the same today, yesterday, and tomorrow. They would talk about a God that talked to them; they just talked like they knew God.

I was one of those alcoholics that never drank until work was done, but when I wasn't working, I was never without a drink.

About this time my wife had been invited to a church that was meeting in an old grocery store building. We went one Sunday morning and there was about 300 people in the place. It was wild. People were clapping their hands along with the music, the music was wild, and they had a band that looked like the bands that played in the "live-music bars"!

Then everything got quiet and I'm looking around and the lady right next to me starts speaking out loud and who knows what she was saying, because she was talking in tongues. My skin was just crawling with goosebumps and the hair on my arms was standing on end. Then a peace kind of came over me and I realized this must be what they were talking about on the radio when they were talking about praying and speaking in tongues!

But you have to know how ignorant I was and how my mind worked in those days. We found out they had a Sunday night service and I thought that was for the people like us who partied and stayed up late on Saturday night. I never realized that these people came to both the Sunday morning service and the Sunday night service!

Also, in this season of time my Aunt Betty Patterson at a family gathering pointed her finger at my chest and said, "Curtis, Jesus loves you!" I would see her smiling face and hear her words every day. I tried to put it out of my mind. Later, I found out she would spend Mondays in her bedroom fasting and praying for the salvation of all our families!

Around the same time, I had an unusual experience one night while in a popular nightclub that was filled with people. At one point I went to use the bathroom and while I'm in there I hear a voice say, "You don't have to do this." I looked around to see who was talking but there was nobody in there except me. I'll never forgot that experience. I believe it was the Lord speaking to me about not having to live this kind of lifestyle of partying.

I was transferred to Minnesota and could no longer listen to the radio station out of Omaha. For the next couple of years, I worked hard and drank even harder. By this time, I was drinking a fifth of whiskey every night.

My wife rededicated her life to the Lord and her attitude and mannerisms drastically changed.

Then on Saturday, June 11th, 1983 a friend of mine picked me up in the morning and we went golfing at the local country club and played 18 holes drinking all along and then we went to a grand opening at a local bar. We closed that place and he pretty much carried me home.

In my drunken state I noticed this booklet that was about 40 pages long titled "It ain't no disease" on the kitchen table. It was a book that said drinking was a choice and one that only I could make and at the end of the book was a "sinner's prayer" and so at 4AM on June 12, 1983 in my living room next to the couch on my knees I prayed this prayer and I was instantly sober and no longer had a desire to drink.

It was here that all old things passed away and all things became new in Christ. I was a new creature and a new person! I did not know that there was a truth in the Bible that said, "If the Son sets you free, you will be free indeed" (John 8:36 NIV). It's been 39 years now since then.

"For whatever a man sows, that he will also reap." (Galatians 6:7b NKJV). This was one of the verses that I believe transformed me. I started choosing to sow good things in my life. I began to look at everything I did and consciously thought what would I reap as a consequence of my actions. I began to live my life by Ephesians 6:8 (NKJV) which says "...whatever good anyone does, he will receive the same from the Lord..."

Over the years since, I went to night school for six years and earned a bachelor's degree in Theology. I've traveled on mission's trips to Colombia, Costa Rica, Moscow, Russia,

Switzerland, France, Peru, Israel, Jordan, Egypt and several trips to Mexico and have many stories I could share. I truly believe that Jesus meant what He said: "I have come that they may have life, and that they may have it more abundantly" (John 10:10 NKJV) and that He wants me to "prosper in all things and be in health, just as your soul prospers" (3 John 2 NKJV).

Prayer: *Heavenly Father, I pray for the addictions in my own life and that of my loved ones to be broken in the powerful name of Jesus.*

3.
I AM VALUABLE

BY YA-LING CHEN
TOKYO, JAPAN

"For by grace you have been saved through faith, and that not of yourselves; it is the gift of God, not of works, lest anyone should boast."

—EPHESIANS 2:8-9 (NKJV)

I have been going to church since I was five years old. I was baptized at age 12. Basically, my whole life I have been a part of church activities and events. I thought that the foundation of my faith was firm and I already knew what Christianity was all about since I had been attending Sunday School, Sunday service, and serving at church events for years.

However, even though I knew the truth that God loves me for who I am, I still couldn't understand personally what that meant for me. I am a single child in the family, but I didn't feel I was loved and accepted because of my gender. (At that time, people in Taiwan still thought boys were more valuable than girls.) From a young age, I learned that love should be earned by good behaviors and outstanding performance. This deep-rooted belief not only affected all my relationships with people, but also my relationship with God.

Based on my incorrect belief, I gradually became a Pharisee-like Christian. I was proud of my good behaviors and devotions to church, and judged people who couldn't reach my religious standard. I had a good reputation at church, but outside of church, I dated non-Christian guys whom I thought could give me the love that my parents didn't fulfill during my childhood. At that time, I never enjoyed the love of God. Instead, I thought there was a huge gap between God and me. I didn't have a true relationship with God and Christianity was merely a religion to me!

Nothing changed until I met a pastor who was from a different denomination. When I listened to his testimonies and stories, I was amazed about his life experiences of following God and his lively relationship with God. I had never seen anyone whose relationship with God was so close in my life! So, I prayed to God, "God, help me have a real relationship with you, just like the pastor does!"

I believe God was pleased with the prayer and He responded to my prayer by leading me to live in different cities and countries since then. After three years, in 2008, He led me to the States and I joined a local Chinese church in Northern California. I started speaking in tongues at a Holy

Spirit conference and since then I've often wept during worship times with the Lord because I've felt His love for me.

I remember one time during a worship conference, when the worship team was leading the old hymn "Jesus loves me", 「主耶穌愛我，主耶穌愛我，主耶穌愛我，有聖經告訴我」 a thought came to my mind that Jesus was there with me when I felt lonely and afraid during my childhood. My tears couldn't stop because I finally realized He has always been with me since I was little!

God not only restored my broken sensor of receiving His love, He also drew me closer to Him. At the beginning, I still used performance-based standards to evaluate myself and others. By serving with others, I realized how arrogant I was and the performance-based standard didn't please God at all.

Finally, I got tired of the standard and questioned myself: I have truly experienced God's love, but why do I still feel distant from God? Did I just try to fulfill myself by serving in different groups and many ministries instead of spending time with Him and knowing His will? Then I said the same prayer to God, " God, please help me have a real relationship with You."

One year later, God led us to Austin, Texas in 2016. With little chance to serve at church, I found that I used to judge my own value and find my sense of security on what I could do or what I have done. Now looking back at that time when we lived in Texas, I am amazed by what God had done in our lives. During that time, my value and security in Him was renewed; furthermore, God also revealed the lies hidden in my life and showed me the truth. The most amazing thing is that He restored our marriage and made our relationship more sincere and stronger than before.

During the four years in Texas without our familiar church life and friends we had in California I sometimes felt like we were walking in the wilderness and experienced some dark nights. However, God replaced what He took away. He is with me all the time and gives me strength to face challenges and difficulties in my daily life. My trust in God is shaped through the environment He provides and my faith grows little by little through the churches He leads me to. Now I have confidence to say that I have a real relationship with God and I am eager to be closer to Him.

Prayer: *Father God, please help me know the value that You have given me. I thank You that I don't have to earn Your love but that You freely give it to me unconditionally. Help me to love others the same way. Amen.*

4.
I HAVE PURPOSE

BY DAICHI KOBAYASHI
TOKYO, JAPAN

"For I know the thoughts that I think toward you, says the Lord, thoughts of peace and not of evil, to give you a future and a hope."

—JEREMIAH 29:11 (NKJV)

My life started to change when my older brother moved to Tokyo and entered a university there. Every time he came back home, he always told me what his life was like in Tokyo. I became jealous of him because we grew up in the countryside and my hometown had nothing attractive for teens. I wanted to get out of the countryside and start a fun and new life in a big city like him. Fortunately, I passed an entrance exam at a university in Tokyo, so I moved there when I was 18. I thought my life would be better.

Everything was new and attractive in Tokyo. I made many new friends and tried whatever I wanted to do. It was a lot of fun. But it didn't last for long. "Things" or "friends" couldn't truly fill me inside. There was always a hole in me. I acted like my life was great and perfect on the outside in front of people, but I was lonely, scared, and worried about my future.

My life got boring because every day was the same—going to school, studying, and going home. I still remember the day when I looked up to the sky and asked, "What is the meaning or purpose of life? Am I just going to work after I graduate from school and wait until I die? Is there something more in this life?" I was walking in the darkness in a big city that never gets dark and looking for something that could be a light in my life.

But one day, an American guy started to talk to me on a train. He needed some help. When he got off the train, he invited me to his friend's housewarming party. I didn't know who he was, but he seemed nice, so I said yes to his invitation and went to the party that weekend. Later I found out that he was a Christian missionary in Japan.

I met a pastor at the party. As I talked with him, I realized that he had something that I didn't have. I wasn't sure what it was, but he looked happy and smiled all the time. So I asked him "Why do you look so happy?" He told me about Jesus. I knew nothing about Christianity at that time so I didn't understand it well. But he was different and his demeanor was attractive, so I started hanging out with him.

I loved hanging out with him because he always loved me for who I was, cared for me, and encouraged me. He didn't care whether I was a Christian or not. Moreover, he always gave me a big hug when we met. We don't have a hugging culture in Japan, so I felt so loved when he hugged me.

Before realizing it, these countless hugs started to melt down my hard heart and I started to think I want to be like him and got interested in knowing what he had. I asked him questions many times. I thank him today that he didn't give up on me even though it took so long. Yes, I finally met God. God showed me that He had good plans for me and to give me a future and a hope.

When I realized this, a light came into my life. God showed me that there is a purpose and meaning in life because God made us special. God turned my boring life into a life where every day I am looking forward to what God is going to do. He filled the hole in my heart. The love of God was the one thing that I was looking for.

There are many people in Japan that are having the same experiences that I had, so I want to show them His love like my pastor did to me and tell them God can be the answer.

Prayer: *Father God, I pray I would know my purpose and identity that You have given me and fulfill it. In Jesus' name I pray, amen.*

5. GOSPEL MUSIC CHANGED MY LIFE

BY JUNKO MOURI
KANAGAWA, JAPAN

"This is what the Lord says, he who made the earth, the Lord who formed it and established it—the Lord is his name: 'Call to me and I will answer you and tell you great and unsearchable things you do not know.'"

—JEREMIAH 33:2-3 (NIV)

My way of life was changed by my encounter with Jesus Christ, and I am still being changed. God has a great plan for me and continues to lead me to a life of hope by giving me new joy and peace of mind.

In the past, I had problems at home and did not talk to anyone about what was on my mind. My relationship with my parents, who were busy working together, was not strong, and I think I did not have much experience with family gatherings.

About the time when I was a teenager, I avoided having close interpersonal relationships because I was too proud to talk with others and had secrets that I did not want to share. In retrospect, I think I was afraid that people would find out the truth about my inner life.

In my 20s, I experienced rock bottom in my relationship with my parents and I was deeply hurt. I did not feel like I was at fault. I blamed my parents and ran away from home. After a big love affair, I got married, moved and changed jobs several times. Even though I had a family, new friendships, good health, and a good job, the secrets of my heart grew and the bad habits remained the same.

The pleasures of daily life were a refreshing change of pace, but at times they left me feeling empty and lonely. I was in physical and mental pain because of a mistake I had made, and I wanted to disappear. I was thinking, "I don't care what happens to my life."

It was around that time that I heard the gospel of Jesus Christ. A friend invited me to go to a church and join a choir that sings gospel music. I ended up going even though I didn't know what it was all about. I went and sat down with the people who had gathered there to sing gospel songs. It was the first time for me to be in an atmosphere where a mass of voices resonated in my heart. I was sweating and tense, and inwardly thought, "I shouldn't have come here." I made a reasonable excuse and left halfway through.

As if drawn to the place, I went to the gospel choir practice. I often wondered how I would feel if I were a Christian. Words like, "What we are doing is sowing seeds," "We are going to share the gospel," "Eternal life," and "Let's share with each other" made an impression on me. They sang the words spoken by Jesus, "I am the way, the truth, and the life." During the prayers and the Bible explanations, I began to feel nervous, but I still wanted to be there.

Little by little, my heart changed. I began to think that I needed Jesus, my Savior, who loved me, died as a substitute for my sins, and rose from the dead, in my life. But how could I go about doing this?

I began to remember how I had deceived and hurt others and hurt myself, thinking that no one would notice. In the past I had believed that no one would ever know how I felt, but now I felt as if a light was shining on me. I cried a lot. And I spent days in which the words "many past mistakes" and "Jesus Christ" and "salvation" seemed to be directly connected and pressed to my heart.

I believed in myself and had been trying to live my life on my own. I had not admitted my mistakes. I complained to the people around me and did not respect my parents. I tried to change them, but it was my stubborn heart that needed to change. Finally, I fervently declared, "I need you, Jesus. Please come into my life."

Since then, in God's reassurance, I have gone through the process of healing my twisted and wounded heart with God's words of love. It was a wonderful gift to admit my mistakes, apologize to my father and mother, and experience reconciliation. Previously, I had sought fleeting pleasures, thinking that emotional pleasure was happiness, but I had been struggling in pain, feeling empty and without meaning in my life. I am so glad that I had this experience of healing in my life.

Living with God is totally different from the values and ways of life in this world! In God is where I find the meaning of being alive. I want to continue to share with my family that there is hope for eternity, and that I will be faithful to live my limited life to the fullest until the day I leave this world.

Prayer: *Father God, You know my heart and my innermost secrets. There's nothing I can hide from You. Heal me. Help me forgive. Give me freedom in Jesus. Amen.*

6.
I'VE MADE UP MY MIND TO FOLLOW JESUS

BY HYUNJI LEE
KANAGAWA, JAPAN

"Again Jesus spoke to them, saying, 'I am the light of the world. Whoever follows me will not walk in darkness, but will have the light of life.'"

—JOHN 8:12 (ESV)

From the time I was very young I had many opportunities to go to church in my home country of Korea; there are more churches there than convenient stores. But I couldn't get myself to come to faith in Jesus or believe in Christianity. To me, Christianity seemed a competition of how to gather more people rather than sharing love and God's words.

I have always wanted to explore who I am and what I live for. I talked a lot about this with my family and we decided to go to a Catholic church. I got baptized there when I was in junior high, but I was merely a Sunday worshiper; I didn't live according to God's words.

I met my boyfriend at university. He is now my husband and a Christian. I respected what he thinks about Christianity and we occasionally went to a Christian church together on Sundays, but still, I didn't have faith. He didn't force me to believe the same religion as him, but waited for me to come to faith on my own. At times I was amazed at his thoughts and behavior as a Christian.

After several years, I had the opportunity to visit my boyfriend's family in Japan around the Christmas holiday. His family is all Christian, and I visited the Japanese church where his family goes. While there, I felt for the first time a calmness and peace in the church.

Several years later we got married and moved to Japan. It was all a new experience for me. I believe I made the best choice to create a new family, but I had to abandon my old life and move to an unfamiliar country where I couldn't speak their native language.

My whole new life started in Japan and I went to that same Japanese church. One of the members could speak English so she taught me about the Bible every Sunday. She helped me to open my mind to Jesus. I was a little bit shocked that the answer I was eager to find about life was all in Jesus! But because that church was in Japanese, I couldn't understand much of the pastor's message.

Meanwhile, there was a classmate at my Japanese school. His name is Ben. At first, I heard he came to Japan to be a missionary but I thought it had nothing to do with my life. But after a few months we managed to move out to Kanagawa and I found out by chance that Ben's church was a few train stations from where I would be living! We were looking for a new church to attend and we finally met Paz Church thanks to Ben.

When I first came to Paz Church it felt so comfortable, like home, because there were many foreigners there who live in Japan just like me and I was able to express my feelings in English. Moreover, every message spoke to my heart and I could feel that this love and joy was what Jesus wanted to share with me. In our church family group, I am starting to get to know about Jesus more and am eager to grow in my relationship with Him.

I've made up my mind to follow Jesus from now on, and I am trying to always be thankful in life.

Prayer: *Father God, I've made up my mind to follow You. There's no turning back for me. I believe in You and trust You with my life.*

7.
"STOP. IT'S NOT WORTH IT."

BY NICK WISNIEWSKI
MICHIGAN, USA

"For I am sure that neither death nor life, nor angels nor rulers, nor things present nor things to come, nor powers, nor height nor depth, nor anything else in all creation, will be able to separate us from the love of God in Christ Jesus our Lord."

—ROMANS 8:38-39 (ESV)

Before I met the Lord, I was in a pretty dark place. I had reached the place internally of believing that I was actually incapable of being loved. I wholeheartedly believed that my worth and value as an individual was tied to my actions.

As I would fail in certain areas, I believed that my ability to be loved by others would lessen more and more each day. It got to the point where I started to contemplate suicide. My thought was that I could never do enough to feel loved, so what was the point?

One particular night, I remember being so overwhelmed with this need to be loved. I had extremely disappointed someone that day. I started preparing to take my life. However, right before that moment came, I heard from the Lord for the first time in my life. Although I didn't know it at the time, I remember the Lord speaking, "Stop. It's not worth it."

Several years later, I was invited to attend a youth group at a local church. I mainly went to get out of the house, or because it was something to do on a Wednesday night. Eventually though, I started paying attention. I started listening about this Jesus, that I had believed to be some distant figure.

I started hearing that Jesus died on the cross to take away my sin. He died on the cross for me. There was a worship song that we played often then. In the bridge of the song the worship leader would sing about grace. Although I had heard this song many times before, I'll never forgot the day something special happened.

An image was thrown into my mind. In this image, I was swimming in the middle of an ocean. I couldn't see any land. All I could see is ocean. I turned around looking for land, but I was completely surrounded by ocean. Then I heard this, "Every drop in this ocean, is a grace for you." Wow. In that moment, I realized that I am completely, entirely surrounded by the love of the Father. I got it. I understood. I surrendered my life to Him in that moment, feeling the complete and perfect love of God.

Over the next few years of learning what it means to live for the Lord, I decided to do a yearlong internship at my church, to aid in the ministry and grow in my faith. This is where I met Leanna, the woman who would become my wife.

When I think about the greatest testimony in my life, I think of love. The Lord brought me out of such a dark place in life. A place where I didn't know love. He then showed me his great and marvelous love for me. He then rooted me deep into a community that is so authentic and real, with true friendship and companionship. Praise the Lord.

Prayer: *Father God, help me to understand, feel, and receive Your love for me today. Amen.*

ENCOUNTERS WITH GOD

8.
A LIGHTNING MOMENT

BY NATE REUTTER
KANAGAWA, JAPAN

"My sheep hear my voice, and I know them, and they follow me."

—JOHN 10:27 (ESV)

One of the greatest discoveries a person has is to discover the reason for which they were born. Some people seem to know from a very young age and others spend their whole lives never really discovering it. For me, it was a lifelong process that eclipsed in a sudden defining moment.

I grew up in a Christian home and my parents encouraged me to try all kinds of different activities and sports. Some of them I enjoyed. Many I did not. But my mom did an amazing job of getting me to try a little bit of everything. Eventually two things stood out: music and math. When it came time to choose a career path, music was the more interesting option but a less solid career path, so I was encouraged to pursue engineering.

And so, I did, and enjoyed it too! At least until I sensed God calling me to full-time ministry. I had sensed it several times before, and even shared this with my parents. Their advice was to get a degree that would lead to a solid full-time secular job but keep serving God in a church. But as I prayed about it for over a year, I sensed more and more that I should pursue ministry—specifically music ministry in a church.

With my parents' blessing, I changed majors and got a music ministry degree from a Bible college. Soon after graduating college, not only did I have a full-time ministry job lined up, but I also met the girl of my dreams. I was sure I was going to marry this wonderful girl named Ruth, but she wasn't! In fact, she made it very clear to me: "I'm only going to marry someone who is called to be a missionary." I had been on some mission trips before, but never before had I seriously considered being a missionary. To me, one would have to be *very* sure that they were called to missions. I knew several missionaries and admired them very much, but I also knew that it was anything but an easy life path.

Ironically, or should I say providentially, my parents had just answered the call to become missionaries themselves and moved to Brazil to serve with PAZ, the same missions organization that Ruth grew up in. Ruth and I just so happened to visit our parents in Brazil over Christmas, me for the first time ever. They both served in the same Brazilian city of Santarém.

I remember walking into the Paz Church for the very first time. Loud, upbeat praise music filled the air. I sensed something so wonderful in that place the likes of which I had never experienced before. I was soon in tears. I heard God speak to me so clearly, "This is what I have for you." It was as if God had hit me with a bolt of purpose and destiny all at once. A lightning moment. A lifetime of prayers seemingly answered in one clarifying moment. Everyone was dancing and praising God. I was a mess of tears, life changed!

That was nearly 20 years ago. Ruth and I got married and have been missionaries with PAZ ever since, first in Brazil and now in Japan. The road to get to where we are today was anything but easy. But through all of life's most difficult situations—the kind that make you want to give up and do something else—I can still clearly remember what God spoke to me in that one defining moment, and it keeps me anchored and on course.

Prayer: *Heavenly Father God, please speak to me today. May I hear Your voice clearly and follow You. In Jesus' name, amen.*

9.
BAPTIZED IN THE SPIRIT IN THE UPPER ROOM

BY ANDREW BENNETT
CALIFORNIA, USA

"And they were all filled with the Holy Spirit and began to speak in other tongues as the Spirit gave them utterance."

—ACTS 2:4 (ESV)

My parents invited me to go to Israel for a Holy Land tour with a pastor named Perry Stone. However, before I jump into this testimony, I want to first set the stage.

I was about 22 or 23 years old at the time and had quit my job about six months prior (after a good friend died) to focus only on seeking God. I had the financial ability to not work and recently had found it hard to find any purpose in working until I could figure out why I was alive.

What happens when I die? The big questions of life that for some reason I had neglected for the first 20 years of my life. I was in a pursuit, not just to learn about God, but to know for sure the truth of what life is about. I was very disciplined and determined. Most mornings I would wake up to just read my Bible. For hours. While friends I knew were going to work, I took seeking God as a job each day.

Reading my Bible, listening to teachings, praying, worshiping, all in my small apartment in Austin, TX. Several nights a week I would attend men's Bible studies, I took a class at University of Texas called Perspectives on the Worldwide Christian Movement, I would walk the streets to hang out with the poor, and accepted invitations from a myriad of people I met along the journey, always diving into deep conversations. My friends watched me change. I noticed myself changing and found lots of freedom along the way. Freedom from girls, from alcohol and partying, from comparison to others. The pursuit of God changed my life and I had great joy and hope for the future. However, what I really wanted was to know if God was real—to experience Him.

Up to that point, everything was a good philosophy that I was really thankful for. But deep down I believed there was more. When my parents invited me to Israel, I was at a point of giving up. Thinking that Christianity was a good philosophy and teaching, but never experiencing the reality of God.

Deciding to go to Israel with Perry Stone would forever change my life. I traveled with a group of about 40 people from site to site on a large bus. I immediately noticed that there was something different about many of the believers I was traveling with. They were so joyful. As we would stop at different sites along the tour, they would shout out words like, "Hallelujah" and "Praise God." They would stop at the most random times and just start to worship Jesus. I thought they were weird, but I was curious and recognized that they seemed to know Jesus better than I did. They had a different type of relationship with Him then I had ever experienced.

One day, I was at lunch with a group when an old lady, a pastor from Maine, mentioned something about the baptism of the Holy Spirit. My ears immediately perked up with curiosity and I asked her what that was. She answered and although I couldn't tell you what she said, I knew I wanted it. When she asked me if I wanted to receive the baptism of the Holy Spirit I said yes, even though I didn't know what exactly it was, and in all honesty, thought I had already received the Holy Spirit. I mean I had been baptized twice already. But I was not content and wanted more—and this seemed like the way to more.

A couple days later our bus stopped at another site. It was the supposed upper room in Jerusalem. As I had become accustomed to, the group stopped and began to sing and worship Jesus. However, this time the lady came up to me and asked if she could pray with me. I said yes and held my hands open as she prayed. She didn't pray long before asking me to pray. I wasn't sure what to pray for so I just started telling God I wanted Him and confessing. I began to repeat the same thing over and over that I wanted God.

My parents were right there when this was happening, which was outside of my comfort level, but I didn't care. My desire to meet God trumped anything else. Before long I started to feel electricity in my hands and feet. It was moving and started to take over my whole body to the point where it was hard to stand.

The people standing around me helped me to the ground where the electricity consumed me. My arms were out and elevated above the ground about two inches, even though I wasn't using my strength to hold them. I was essentially in the shape of a cross lying there on the ground in the upper room. I then started to feel what I later described as nails going through my arms. Yet, it didn't hurt. And I started to speak in another language. (There may have been someone speaking in tongues in my ear, I'm not certain.)

While I'm not sure how long I was lying on the ground, when I eventually stood up, I continued to feel the electricity in my hands for another 30 minutes or so. My mom had a slight cold at the time and took my hands and put them on her neck. She said she immediately felt better. The entire experience was heavenly.

When I went back to my hotel room that night I kept replaying over and over what had happened. And wondering if the language I had spoken had left me. But when I would open my mouth to speak, I could still speak this mystery language, I later learned was tongues.

I had been reading my Bible in chronological order and decided to pick up where I last left off. It happened to be

Acts chapter 2, where it talks about the day of Pentecost where the believers were all gathered together in the upper room. The Holy Spirit filled them and they all began speaking in other languages as the Holy Spirit empowered them.

I couldn't believe it. I was reading the exact story that had just happened to me. It truly felt like I was seen by God. His timing was perfect. I stopped doubting if God was real or not and knew that I was exactly where I was supposed to be. When I read my Bible that night it felt like I was reading for the first time. Like a veil had been removed from my eyes. It was divine.

Heading back to Austin, Texas after this trip, I wasn't sure what life was going to be like. Everything seemed to have changed yet I was excited about the future. I went back to some of the men's Bible studies excited to share about what had happened. However, the responses I received were not as I was expecting.

I thought people would be amazed and would want to hear and talk more about it. Plus, I had more questions than ever and needed people to talk with. I knew I needed to find people who could help walk me through what I had just experienced and started looking for a new church.

A friend told me about a church called Glad Tidings. When I showed up on Sunday morning for the first time, I was sought out by who I later learned was the youth pastor. He invited me to go for a hike with him where we talked for hours. He also spoke in tongues and had been baptized in the Holy Spirit so he was able to relate to what I had just been through. He invited me to attend a prayer meeting, the hour before his youth event.

When I showed up, the room was dark, worship music was blaring, and people were walking around praying out loud. Once again, I was completely out of my comfort level as I had never experienced a prayer meeting like this. But I pushed myself and opened up my hands, closed my eyes, and began to talk to Jesus. To my surprise, as it had happened in Israel, electricity started to fill my hands and I became bold. To me, it was confirmation once again that I was in the right place. While the questions have never stopped, I have stopped questioning whether or not God is real. My life became his ever since that day in the Upper Room.

***Prayer:** Father God, baptize me with Your Holy Spirit. In Jesus' name, amen!*

10.
GOD IS AN AWESOME DAD:
RAISING CHILDREN THROUGH TRAUMA AND PAIN

BY CHRISTINE HUBER
KANAGAWA, JAPAN

"I will be a Father to you, And you shall be My sons and daughters, Says the Lord Almighty."

—2 CORINTHIANS 6:18 (NKJV)

My first husband, Luke, and I were missionaries in the Amazon for 18 years, introducing many people to Jesus. Together with our two daughters and two sons, we lived and traveled on our houseboat sometimes months at a time, visiting the river villages. To this day we have innumerably wonderful memories, and many scary ones too... days I thought would be our last. But God saved us every time.

Our children loved visiting the small homes, making new friends, inviting them to see our Jesus films, or attend meetings about the love of Jesus. We also gave out simple medicines and bandages to those who came to our boat. The kids loved hunting ducks and spearfishing, and roasting our catch on fires we made on the beach. We even speared alligators to eat. They loved canoeing, swimming behind the boat, helping Dad fix the houseboat motor, or tying us up to trees to pass the night, rocking in the waves.

One day tragedy struck, and it appeared that God did not save us from danger. Our daddy crashed his small ultralight experimental floatplane into a huge lake that empties out into the Amazon River, a place where we had several churches started. He died on impact. It was actually his third crash. The other two times he should have died too, but God miraculously spared his life. This time he was gone.

It was August 4, 1994. He was 44 years old. Our adventurous husband, daddy, and church leader suddenly disappeared from our lives. We were grief-stricken beyond explanation. Besides dealing with the grief myself, I didn't know how to be a "mom and a dad" for my children. Isaiah was only 10, and Josiah was 13. Esther was 18, and Sarah was 19.

My future seemed very bleak. I spent hours alone with God in my tiny attic every morning, crying and talking to God, reading my Bible, writing confidential notes to God, singing endless worship songs with my little guitar. Through His Word, He asked me to believe Him!

Even though my circumstances all around me certainly did not look good, He asked me to have patience. God heard my cries. With patience I received so many answers to my confidential prayers! I experienced the truth that God really is alive! He was listening to me! He daily did little miracles for me and my children that I did not expect. I could actually leave the attic each day with a huge sigh of relief.

I was so amazed by the miracle God performed in my heart—such a feeling of peace and hope, and new excitement for another day. I could take care of my children and visit my neighbors too. Many of them had worse problems than we had, and eventually many came to know the love of Jesus.

One lady, however, complained. She said it looked like I didn't love my husband. I didn't wear black, and I was constantly looking okay, and even smiling. I had to shake my head with a genuine smile from my heart. I said, "No! It's not because I didn't love my husband! It's because God did not die!"

One day I went up the stairs to our bedroom. At the very top was a huge, bigger-than-life size poster of the two of us. Luke had made it when we got engaged. He posted it in our house many years ago. We had been married for 21 beautiful years. I looked at his face on the poster, and I said to him in my mind, (knowing he couldn't hear me), "Luke, you left me! You promised you would help me finish raising our boys. But as I told you, I don't know how to be a mom and a dad!" He couldn't answer, of course. But God, very clearly and lovingly in my mind, said, "Christine dear, you are not a mom and a dad! You are a mom, and I am the dad! I am going to raise your children even better than you can imagine!" What a relief came over me! "Oh, thank You, God! I am not a mom and a dad! I am just a mom! You are the dad, and You are going to raise my children even better than I can imagine. But I have huge imaginations for my children!"

I always remembered that promise, especially when tough times came, through all the many difficulties that we faced in the years to come. One evening, I surprisingly got a very unexpected phone call from Luke's younger brother Tim, an amazing single missionary in Japan, for over 10 years. He asked me to pray about marrying him and helping him with church-planting in Japan. This was such an exciting proposal, I was overwhelmed with God's love for me to give me another awesome missionary husband, so dedicated to serving Him and never giving up.

My biggest challenge was knowing that the spiritual warfare in Japan would probably be tougher for me than in Brazil. In Japan, unlike Brazil, very few people were turning to Jesus. For years, the percentage of evangelical Christians was still at 0.5 percent of the population. I heard that many missionaries had become discouraged and given up. It would be tough spiritual warfare. With the encouragement and support of our parents and our children, we got married.

Our first daughter, Sarah, was married and studying to be a missionary nurse. Our second daughter, Esther, was in Bible college, also preparing to be a missionary. Our two sons were still teenagers, Josiah, 17, and Isaiah, 14 years old at the time. I brought them to Japan, thinking that they would love it. However, the adjustments were much bigger than I could have ever imagined. Besides adjusting to the sight of their mom in love with their new stepdad, Tokyo was completely opposite from the Amazon.

The boys did not know the language or have any friends. We lived in a two-room very small apartment inside the church. The culture was opposite from where they grew up, with many strict rules that needed to be precisely followed. They were living in a new jungle, not of trees but of concrete buildings. Worst of all, they suffered bullying. They tried so hard to adjust, doing all they knew or could even imagine to do, but soon they began suffering some very confusing emotions. As a mom, I was in agony, thinking it was all my fault. I didn't know what to do. Sometimes in the middle of the night, I couldn't sleep. I would bow down with my face on the floor and remind God, saying, "Remember, God, You are the Dad! Please help me!" He would answer in my mind, "Say, 'thank you'! I have amazing plans for your boys! They are going to be okay! Just wait!"

Wondering why God was putting us through all this, I obeyed and I thanked Him over and over for the agonizing times we were going through. Every time I thanked God, it was incredible how He would then bring indescribable peace to my heart. I waited for many years, praying, believing, and doing all we could to help them out. Now, 28 years later, I can say with tears running down my cheeks, "Thank You Father! You are always right. You are an awesome Dad!"

All four of our children married awesome Christian spouses, and have given us eleven precious grandchildren. They are giving their whole lives to serving God and people. They know God is their real Dad. When they have pain and problems they know where to run. It's so touching to me to see them teaching our grandchildren to love and depend on their Father God too. Each year that passes, I become even more surprised. God has given each of our children and their spouses such crazy passion for forwarding His Kingdom, bringing hope to those without Jesus, and raising up leaders to be church-planters. Our children and their beautiful families live in different parts of the world, lovingly and tirelessly sacrificing themselves, bringing people to Jesus.

As a family, they all love and highly honor their stepdad Tim, who is also a very fun and adventurous grandpa to all our grandchildren. We can't thank God enough for giving him to us! "Thank You God! You are such an amazing Dad! You have raised our children far better than I could have ever imagined!" God is an awesome Dad, not only for them, but for you and for me too!

Prayer: *Heavenly Father God, You are such a good Father. Thank You for taking care of me and my family. In Jesus' name, amen.*

MIRACLES

11.
JUST MOVE

BY D. KIRK
USA BASED MINISTRY

---

*"Trust in the Lord with all your heart,
and lean not on your own understanding;
in all your ways acknowledge Him,
and He shall direct your paths."*

—PROVERBS 3:5-6 (NKJV)

We are a ministry that involves traveling at least six months of each year. This has been our lifestyle for over 30 years. However, what do you do when God tells you to move and governments say you can't. When your own government says, "If you, or anyone, leaves it is prison or a massive fine." When the nation you are going to says, "If you come, we won't let you in." We knew of others who had lawyers to act on their behalf but were still forbidden to leave.

Do you obey the voice of God or the threats of man? That was our predicament, although not really a predicament—we obey God!

So, we set out for the airport with our suitcases, passports, and documents we thought might help us. We were carefully prepared to head to the nation that had asked us to come. On arriving we saw police cars lined up ensuring no one would be leaving. We got out of the car and walked through the middle of them and into the airport. It was a huge airport, but we saw no one except airport officials and police. Looking over at the check-in desks we only saw one open, one person behind the desk and no one in front.

So, we walked over and handed in our passport. Our cases were sent down the conveyer belt and we were handed our tickets—no questions asked, not even "did you pack your own bags." With tickets in hand we headed to security, our tickets were checked, and through we went.

We were totally at peace but at the same time it seemed surreal. "Time for coffee", we thought, so we headed to the lounge where our passports and tickets were checked again. Then came what we thought would be the biggest hurdle—getting through the gate for boarding.

Again, our passports and tickets got checked and on the plane we went. By now I was thinking that maybe this would be like shoplifting where the authorities wait until you have left the store before arresting you and that when we boarded the airplane the hand of the earthly law would descend—but the plane took off with us on it! As we watched the ground disappearing and a nation trapped within its borders the enormity of what had happened became a reality. We had escaped!

We had to transit though a neighbouring country and the same thing happened. Again, we had no questions and a smooth transit to yet another part of the journey that was forbidden by earthly authority. The same thing happened as well as we entered the country to which we were headed; even though it was forbidden by the government we were able to enter.

What had happened seemed very "normal." We did not have huge surges of faith, no word that propelled us forward, just the thought "Let's have a go!" It is time for a people to rise up and "Have a go."

So, what happened? We don't know except it seemed that God blinded the eyes of officials. They did not "see" us. God made a way where there was no way. All we had to do was "move."

John Maxwell did a survey on what the common denominator for every miracle was. It was simple! The common denominator was—a problem! Every problem is a miracle waiting to happen. Just move!

***Prayer:** Father God, help me move in faith to where You are leading me!*

12.
FINALLY PREGNANT

BY COLLEEN SHORE
KANAGAWA, JAPAN

"Like arrows in the hands of a warrior are children born in one's youth."

—PSALM 127:4 (NIV)

For as long as I can remember I always wanted to have children of my own. It was a desire that only became stronger after my husband and I married in our early 30's. We spent the first few years of our marriage extremely busy with work and renovating our new home so we decided to put off having children.

Then unexpectedly in the middle of the chaos, almost two years into our marriage, we became pregnant! Though it was a surprise, we became excited for the little one to join our lives. However, the joy was short lived as early in the pregnancy I had a miscarriage. I was shocked by the grief I felt for this little life that had only been with us a short time.

About a year after this experience my husband and I started to discuss the idea of trying to have a baby. The conversation was difficult for both of us because we could see how adding a child to our lives was going to be complicated. We had already started getting ready for a move to Japan and pregnancy and delivery seemed to add extra variables neither one of us was ready for. We decided to move forward with having a child but after over a year with no success we became concerned.

Our departure date for Japan was coming up within a few months and access to specialists in Canada takes time. During this time, I feel that God was orchestrating getting the medical care that I needed. Usually, it takes a year to see a specialist and then another six months or more to wait for any surgery that you need. God paved a way for me to see a specialist within a month.

I was diagnosed with endometriosis and was able to have two surgeries a month later. My final procedure happened a week before we had to fly out to Japan. The procedures were successful and the specialists had told me that I had good chances of now becoming pregnant!

Overjoyed, I fully expected things to move forward quickly. However, after our move, it felt like it wasn't going to happen and I became distraught and unable to feel joy for others who were pregnant. Each month ticked by with tears as it seemed my heart's desire would remain unfulfilled. It felt like time was not on our side; we seemed to be only getting older.

We shared our story with close friends and family, asking for prayer that God would help us have a child. Many prayed with us. Some shared their own stories of struggle. It was always emotional.

Then three years after my miscarriage I was crying tears of joy rather than sadness, we were pregnant! Today I am six months pregnant and every time I feel the kick in my belly I thank the Lord and pray for the continued health of our baby.

During this process God has taught me two things. First, God has placed community around us for a reason. During our struggle with fertility, it was so helpful to bare our burden with other Christians and have them pray for us. God placed an understanding community around us to comfort and lift us up. If the circumstances had turned out different and we were never able to have a child, I know that God and our community would have provided a safe place for us to heal in.

Lastly, God taught me that His timing is perfect and it was evident in so many ways. After reflecting on our fertility struggles, both my husband and I recognized that it would have been very hard to move to Japan with a newborn and that the dream of living in Japan may never have come to be. Also, the time without a child gave me the opportunity to care for my father while he had stage 4 cancer (thankfully he is in remission now). Additionally, God's timing was perfect as he orchestrated getting me the medical care I needed with amazing speed. I think I finally realize that God's timing is always better than my timing.

I pray that this testimony encourages you to continue to pray and have faith in God's provision and his perfect timing!

Prayer: *Father God, I trust Your provision and Your timing. I pray Your will would be done in my life. In Jesus' name, amen.*

13.
MIRACLE IN BELIZE

BY MICHAEL MAHER
MISSOURI, USA

"It is the Lord who goes before you. He will be with you; he will not leave you or forsake you. Do not fear or dismayed."

—DEUTERONOMY 31:8 (ESV)

I was in Belize with a ministry that distributes Bibles and Christian educational material to third world countries. We were doing special healing and salvation crusades where we distributed Bibles. We were slated to speak at the nation's naval base on the other side of the country from where we were staying, and when we showed up the Navy was busy practicing a presidential parade or something official of that manner and we were not permitted to enter.

We had US military men with us who were going to share the Word of the Lord with the Belizean soldiers. Our real hope was to go to the army base, but the naval base was the only one that had said we could come. Now that we were stuck after a four- or five-hour drive with no place to preach, we decided to dip into a hotel's restaurant and pray and have breakfast.

While in there praying, the Prime Minister of Belize's son came in for breakfast. He also happened to be the Ambassador of Music for the nation. His name is Shyne and he was a member of Bad Boy Records and very well known in the Hip Hop community. Because I was a musician, the leader of our trip boldly walked me over to Shyne, the Prime Minister's son, and said to him clearly and concisely our situation and asked if he'd like me to sit with him for breakfast since we were both into music.

So I'm sitting there at breakfast with a super famous rapper, who happens to be a dignitary's son, and sharing my music and breakfast with him. He coolly walks over to our trip leader after eating and said he'd escort us to the military base! The very place we were hoping to go in the first place! He walked us right up to the gate and the guards held up their guns and shouted, "Hey! Stop!" Shyne kept walking and said, "Open the gate." When they recognized him, they hurried to open the gates for us. They all looked at him star-struck and I heard a bunch of them saying, "It's Shyne!"

Shyne had the man in charge gather every soldier he could for an impromptu meeting. We ministered music and the Word to the soldiers and the presence of God was there. The US Army men who were with us brought a cut-to-the-heart word. Many soldiers were crying, including a British soldier who was sitting in the side corner. Many men responded to the call for salvation and many received Bibles. It was pretty incredible that after thinking we wasted a five-hour drive, the Lord responded to our prayer of faith and not giving up, and gave us an escort to the place we dreamed of going—even better than what we planned! It was the best-case scenario. God is with us!

Prayer: *Lord, I pray for those all around me who don't know You to come into a beautiful relationship with You. Help me have the courage to share You with others. Open doors of opportunity for me to share You with others. In Jesus' name, amen.*

14.
MIRACLE STORY ON THE AMAZON

BY BECKY HRUBIK
PARÁ, BRAZIL

"Heal the sick, cleanse the lepers, raise the dead, cast out demons. Freely you have received, freely give."

—MATTHEW 10:8 (NKJV)

A group of us had gone to the river town of Obidos to help build our church. One afternoon, missionary Mike heard some weird noises from a nearby wooden house that was up on stilts.

Because he didn't speak Portuguese, he called me to go to the house with him. The door was closed, so we knocked. No one answered, but the noises were very clearly coming from the living room. We could see below the floorboards that there was a chain coming out of the living room floor and padlocked to a big rock on the ground. We could not get in.

We waited until after work hours, and sure enough, a young man went into the house. Right away we went and talked with him and asked him what was going on. He had us go into the living room where his mother was sitting in a hammock, with her ankle chained. He explained that his mother was crazy and so he left her every day chained to the floor while he went to work. We asked him if we could pray for her.

As we stood by her side, I asked her what her name was. The demons kept answering all kinds of things—most of it unintelligible. I finally just got her face in my hands and said, "I don't want the demons to speak. I want to talk to this lady. What is your name?" Finally, I understood her say, "Clara." I started to minister to Clara, explaining that Jesus wanted to free her.

Once I felt that she was hearing me, then we cast out the demons in the name of Jesus! That evening, Clara was completely set free. Her son unchained her. She was a new woman!

We left the town the next day, but later received the wonderful news that Clara was going to church with her son and was a completely freed woman! Praise the Lord!

Prayer: *Heavenly Father, You are more powerful than anything on earth. And You have given me authority to advance Your Kingdom. Help me walk in that authority today. Amen.*

15.
TRUSTING GOD WITH YOUR CHILDREN

BY PABLO & ANDREA CAMPOS
MICHIGAN, USA

"Behold, children are a heritage from the Lord, The fruit of the womb is a reward."

—PSALM 127:3 (NKJV)

One of the most profound miracles we have experienced in our family is that of how God has moved in and through the life of our youngest son, Noah. He was diagnosed with autism spectrum disorder, a sensory disorder, and a mixed receptive-expressive speech disorder when he was four years old.

A long time before he was diagnosed, we experienced a multitude of challenges that caused our family to feel trapped and defeated, as if we were in bondage. There were so many places we could not go and activities we could not participate in because we knew many of those situations would trigger Noah to have a meltdown—something that was physically, emotionally, and spiritually overwhelming for the family as a whole.

Soon after our suspicions were confirmed that our son was not neurotypical, I went forward for prayer, and the pastor's wife prayed Genesis 8:1 over my family and me: "But God remembered Noah and all the wild animals and livestock with him in the boat. He sent a wind to blow across the earth, and the floodwaters began to recede" (NLT).

As she prayed God's word over me, God spoke a promise to me. He encouraged me that we (my family) were in the boat with Noah (our son), going through the flood with him, that He was about to the send the wind of His Spirit to blow across the situation and cause the floodwaters to begin to recede. And then He said "But first, let the waters do their work."

The "floodwaters" which were the difficulties presented by Noah's different disorders did not recede immediately, but God began to use the incredibly challenging situation to grow our family closer to Him and each other as we continued to seek Him in prayer for wisdom, guidance and breakthrough. He used us to encourage other families of special needs children to press in and trust God and love like Jesus.

Over the past several years, Noah has experienced one breakthrough after another. He has experienced God working on his behalf to help him to overcome things that seemed impossible, and today, he is an 11 ½ year old boy with great faith in a miracle working God, and he regularly shares his testimony with others about how God has helped him with his disorders so they might know God and trust Him for salvation.

Prayer: *Father God, I thank You that children are a blessing from You. I pray for protection over the children of the world today and for them to find You. In Jesus' name, amen.*

16.
MIRACLE ON THE LAKE

BY BILL TVEDT
IOWA, USA

"Therefore they stayed there a long time, speaking boldly in the Lord, who was bearing witness to the word of His grace, granting signs and wonders to be done by their hands."

—ACTS 14:3 (NKJV)

In 1982 I was a student at Oral Roberts University. One weekend, three of my college friends and I went water skiing on Lake Tenkiller in Oklahoma. We stopped on a small island in the middle of the lake for a lunch break. When we returned to the boat, we realized the key had been left on and the battery was dead. We had no oars and the lake was rough from the wind. We realized we were the only ones on the lake that day and in that moment, we knew we needed a miracle.

We laid hands on the boat and prayed that God would recharge the battery which was clearly dead. After a few moments of praise and prayer, we turned the key and the boat started and the battery registered on the gauge as fully charged!

The next day I was on the phone with my mom and she asked if I had been in some kind of trouble the day before. The Lord had spoken to her that something was wrong and she began to pray in the Holy Spirit for my protection and help. I praise God for the Holy Spirit's power to speak to my mother and her obedience to pray and to be part of that miracle.

Prayer: *Heavenly Father God, thank You for watching over me and protecting me and my loved ones. Amen.*

17. GOD STARTED OUR ENGINE

BY JOSIAH HUBER
KANAGAWA, JAPAN

"And God was doing extraordinary miracles by the hands of Paul."

—ACTS 19:11 (ESV)

When I was younger, my family and I lived in the Amazon jungle of Brazil as missionaries. At different periods we would live on a boat for as long as several months at a time. We had a small speedboat with an outboard engine as well that we would sometimes take with us.

One time my dad and I went out spearfishing together on a place we called "Rock Island." We were in our small speedboat that took gasoline to run. When we were done spearfishing, we headed back to our bigger boat but within about one minute our engine died and we quickly glided to a stop.

My dad pumped the primer to get more gas in the engine and it would start for a second or two but then quickly died again. At this point, he picked up the gas tank and leaned it back and forth but he couldn't hear anything moving. So he took the top off and looked inside and sure enough it was dry. As he pumped the primer it wouldn't grab any gasoline because it was all gone.

My dad laid his hands on our outboard engine and prayed over it. Afterwards, he pulled the rope and the engine started right up. My dad just looked over at me and smiled. We knew it was the Lord that did a miracle for us.

We then traveled back to our bigger boat where we were staying and arrived probably less than 10 minutes later. When we were almost to our boat, my dad revved up the engine some more to go a little faster and toward the very end the engine died on us and we coasted toward our boat. If we would've had to paddle back from the island it would've taken us hours. That day our engine ran on air!

Prayer: *Heavenly Father God, thank You for watching over us every moment of every day. You care about us and every little detail. And You want to be a part of our lives. Help me to trust You with the big things as well as the little things. I love you. In Jesus' name, amen.*

PHYSICAL HEALINGS

18.
I PRAYED TO A GOD I DIDN'T EVEN KNOW YET

BY MATT PARKS
MICHIGAN, USA

"He himself bore our sins in his body on the tree, that we might die to sin and live to righteousness. By his wounds you have been healed."

—1 PETER 2:24 (ESV)

I was adopted by great parents shortly after birth. When I was about four years old, I realized why some of my friends looked like one parent or another and I didn't. I then prayed to a God I didn't even know yet. I asked that when I got older, I would have a child that looked just like me. I somehow knew the answer was "yes."

As I got older, I remember going to a doctor and he said I might not be able to have children. However, I remembered

God's promise. When I got married and then Kris got pregnant, I thanked God for that promise.

When Michael was born, he was stuck in the birth canal too long. He finally was delivered, but couldn't breathe very well. I heard the enemy say to my mind "He is born, and he looks just like you... but now I am taking him." I knew God would not fulfill any promise that way, so I rejected that statement and went to pray over him in the NICU.

There were many monitors and alarming "signs" and I didn't understand them. One was oxygen saturation. It should read 100% or close to it, but Michael's was around the low 60's. I had simply asked a nurse about that and what it meant. She replied that the low number would lead to brain damage or maybe death.

I put my hand on him and said "In the name of Jesus, be healed." The number immediately jumped to mid 70%. Knowing that was still too low, I repeated the prayer the same way, and the number jumped to high 80's. It was still too low but much better. I repeated the prayer, but added "breathe normally." Up until this time Michael had been hyperventilating, among other things. Again, immediately, Michael took a huge deep breath and let it out slow. The number went to 100%. He was healed, he looks just like me, (so does my daughter Daisy) and he has been remarkably healthy in life.

Prayer: *Heavenly Father, thank You that You still heal people today. I pray for healing in my own body and those of my loved ones in Jesus' name, amen.*

19.
GOD HEALED OUR DRUMMER

BY PRADEEPAN JEEVA
WASHINGTON, USA

"But He was wounded for our transgressions, He was bruised for our iniquities; the chastisement for our peace was upon Him, and by His stripes we are healed."

—ISAIAH 53:5 (NKJV)

In 2000, I played bass guitar for a Christian band in Minnesota called, "Innocent Charm." We performed in a competition and won first place so some of us jokingly referred to ourselves as the "Best Christian Band in Minnesota." According to students in New Prague Middle School, we were voted the #1 band, but this is a testimony about the goodness of God and not the sickness of our beats.

Before playing one of our largest concerts at a camp, our drummer, Austin, broke his foot. The day before our show, he tried stopping a boat from crashing into a dock with his leg, and his foot got seriously injured. After the x-rays confirmed his broken bone and the doctor placed his right foot in a cast, Austin showed up to our concert unable to hit the kick drum.

We didn't know what to do. Do we cancel the show and deprive hundreds of young people of our beautiful melodies? Do we replace our drummer?

In our confusion, our guitarist said, "Let's pray God heals his foot!" With only two hours until showtime, we placed our hands on Austin and prayed for supernatural healing in the name of Jesus.

Austin said he felt a warmth and we collectively asked him to take off his cast and try walking. He gave it his best try, and not only was he able to walk—He leaped with joy! Our band stood in awe of the loving and generous healing power of God. God answered the prayers of young people innocent and desperate enough to ask for help in an impossible and somewhat ridiculous situation.

Sadly, that was the last year our band held the "Best Christian Band in Minnesota" title, but the memory of God's healing act remains.

Prayer: *Father God, I pray for those needing healing around me and ask You to touch them with Your miraculous power. In Jesus' name, amen.*

20.
GOD HEALED MY DAUGHTER

BY MIRIAN ALMEIDA
PARÁ, BRAZIL

"Jesus Christ is the same yesterday, today, and forever."

—HEBREWS 13:8 (NKJV)

Soon after our first daughter was born, we experienced a miracle from God.

My daughter, Priscilla, who was ten months old at the time, suddenly became ill with a fever and a lot of diarrhea. We went with her to the hospital several times and sometimes she was hospitalized for treatment.

We suffered a great deal because the doctors could not find out what that was causing the diarrhea. Priscilla was fading. She became weak and pale and couldn't even sit up anymore.

We were in the hospital one afternoon and everything seemed chaotic around us. A child very close to where we were died, and her mother was wailing and crying out for her daughter's life. Other children were in critical states.

That hospital didn't have an ICU or even enough medicine for all those children. I saw the nurses anxious and tense, not knowing what to do. Some of the parents that were there with their sick children were helping the nurses because there weren't enough nurses for all the sick children.

Meanwhile, Priscilla was in a bed, motionless, without reaction and without strength. I cried, not knowing what to do.

That's when my husband arrived and I cried out to him, "Please do something! Let's get our daughter out of here!" He looked at me sad. What could we do? We couldn't take her home like that. I was already so tired because it had been two months and Priscilla had only gotten worse.

It was at that moment that I took her in my arms and we left through a hall in the hospital, not knowing exactly what we were going to do. I saw another small hallway and a door. And without knowing where it led, we went through the door. We found ourselves in a place where all the hospital waste was placed in large black bags.

And there, in the middle of the garbage, with our daughter in our arms, we said a prayer and asked God to do something for us, because we didn't know what else to do.

Suddenly we were led by the Holy Spirit to sing. We started singing loudly. We sang spiritual warfare songs, we sang praises. I don't know exactly how long we stayed there, but it was a long time with many songs.

Priscilla was totally fragile and skinny; she couldn't even move her head. We walked back and forth in the small space we had, sometimes in her father's arms, sometimes in mine. Until at one point a great peace filled our hearts. Then her father said: "Priscilla is healed."

I went back to the room with Priscilla. That night she didn't have a fever, the diarrhea stopped, and she started eating again.

When the doctor arrived in the morning, she was surprised to see how Priscilla's appearance had completely changed.

Due to the need to vacate beds for other children, Priscilla was discharged that morning, but told to return to the hospital if she got worse again. But thank God that wasn't necessary.

A few days later my mother, Priscilla's grandmother, saw her recovering so well! With tears in her eyes she confessed, "I thought Priscilla wouldn't survive." Jesus healed her completely! All glory to Him!

Prayer: *Father God, I pray for Your protection and divine health over me and my family! Amen.*

21.
GOD HEALED A GIRL'S WRIST

BY BRUNO SENE
SÃO PAULO, BRAZIL

"Now to each one the manifestation of the Spirit is given for the common good."

—I CORINTHIANS 12:7 (NIV)

There were some apostles preaching about words of knowledge and the gifts of the ministry here in Brazil. And afterwards we went to the streets to pray for people and hear from the Lord.

I met a girl and her mom. I felt from the Lord that the girl had something going on in her wrist. So, I asked her if she had some pain or problem in her wrist. And she looked at her mom like, "Wow, what is this guy saying?!"

She had her hand covered with some clothes and she took it off and had a big smile and said she has tendinitis. Because of this condition and the inflammation and the pain she was not able to work anymore.

I said let me pray for you. And I shared with her about Jesus and what he did here on the earth and that we could do the same thing and prayed for her. She was instantly healed!

I asked her to take the brace off that was there protecting her arm from sudden movements and she started moving her hand. She started laughing in front of her mom and saying that she felt better and that there was no more pain at all.

I asked her if she had the pain before and she said it was hurting so much. She was so excited about it! So, I told her more about Jesus. She ended up sharing that she was a Jew and I explained that Jesus was a Jew too and that he is the Messiah!

Prayer: *Heavenly Father God, help me to impact others in a powerful way. Lead me by Your Holy Spirit. In Jesus' name, amen.*

22.
RUN AT YOUR GOLIATH

BY LUCAS FORSTHOFF
MICHIGAN, USA

"As Goliath moved closer to attack, David quickly ran out to meet him."

—I SAMUEL 17:48 (NLT)

In 2015, I was dealing with some health issues. I actually thought things were fairly normal with me but as the year went on, I began to notice that I could not get healthy.

I kept battling one bladder infection after the next. I would go to the doctors and get an antibiotic for a bladder infection and after a couple weeks, I would feel better but then about a month later I would get another one. I began to notice my body kept getting bladder infections and it would become so predictable that I would try and get an antibiotic from my doctor before I went on vacation or a mission's trip to anticipate another bladder infection.

I started to feel a large ball deep inside my bladder develop and whenever I leaned over, I could feel that hard ball press against my insides. It was very unnerving to say the least.

I remember the last time going to my doctor and she noticed my health history. She asked me how many bladder infections I had within the last year. I estimated around seven and she began to murmur under her breath, "Oh, that's not good."

In my mind I would rationalize them by blaming them on being in a hot tub or eating too much spicy food, but my doctor would respond to me by saying those things don't typically give you bladder infections.

She started running some extensive tests on me in her office and found some alarming things. She found a large bump on my prostate. I will never forget what she said to me next. She said, "All my patients are apples and you're an orange."

My doctor began to explain to me that it is not normal for a young man such as myself to have this many bladder infections and it is also not normal for her to find such a large bump on a prostate of such a young man. She left the room for a bit and while she was gone, scheduled me to go see four different specialists.

I would learn that these four specialists were essentially a man's worst nightmare. These visits were going to be so bad and so embarrassing that my doctor didn't want to explain the procedures to me for fear of me chickening out and not going.

I left her office dejected, fearful, and devastated. My doctor couldn't say the word cancer to me because no results had come back yet but she was alluding to cancer a lot during our visit.

I remember going home and telling my wife and crying. I couldn't believe I was dealing with something like this at such a young age.

That weekend just so happened to be our church's Men's Conference. Needless to say, I did not feel like going. I was scheduled to host the weekend and I was in charge of many different aspects for the weekend, one of them being a hype man during the conference as I emceed the experience.

I did not feel like going; I did not feel hyped or excited or full of faith for the weekend ahead. I went Friday night to the Men's Conference and told no one about my doctors visit.

I was stuck in my head with thoughts of fear as I anticipated the four different doctors' visits. I couldn't worship and I couldn't pay attention to the preacher that night. I was battling my thoughts and emotions and barely had anything left over to be at church and pay attention.

I went back to the conference on Saturday morning and still felt dejected. After the first main session, we had breakouts and I went to a breakout with the topic of David and Goliath.

I was late into the breakout room and there was one seat left at the front row. I sat down and the preacher began to teach us. Nothing was different and I know the story of David and

Goliath but the preacher said a sentence that was directly from God to me. He said, "David ran at Goliath."

When he said those words, it was as if God spoke directly to me. God wanted me to run at this giant like David did. God also spoke to me that He would heal me as I went.

I knew God wanted me to attack my fears and this thing called cancer as David attacked Goliath, so that's what I did.

I went to my first appointment which was painful and embarrassing. As I drove home, I felt 25% better. I felt a bit stronger and a bit healthier. I went to my second appointment and when I left, I felt 50% better. I scheduled my 3rd appointment and when I left, I felt 75% better.

I had not felt this good in a long time. Feeling 75% healthy almost felt like I was completely healed. I had lived for so long feeling sick that I forgot what it was like to feel completely healthy.

As it turned out, my last appointment was the worst doctors visit of all. I was most scared of this doctor. I started to tell myself, "I don't need to go, I feel great," and I even told my wife I was thinking about cancelling the last doctors visit because I felt so good.

My wife didn't think that was such a good idea and began to remind me that God wanted me to go to all four doctors and I needed to go and get my total healing. I reluctantly agreed with her and scheduled the visit.

I went a few days later and was very nervous sitting in his office waiting for him to come in. I'll never forget what the doctor said when he came inside the room. He said, "I'm surprised you showed up, most men chicken out." I responded, "my wife made me come." He laughed and it somehow made me feel better.

The doctor checked me out and he actually said, everything looks great, I don't see anything wrong with you. It was such a relief to hear him tell me that. I drove home from his office feeling 100% better and I have been healthy ever since.

I don't know why God chose to heal me like this, but He did, and I am glad He did. I have found that obeying God is best and His ways are much different than our ways but if we would simply humble ourselves and follow Him, He will take care of us.

Prayer: *Heavenly Father God, I humble myself before You. Give me the courage to run at my giants and defeat them. Strengthen me and give me victory. In Jesus' name I pray, amen.*

23.
"GET UP, YOU'RE HEALED."

BY KRISTIN VAN VLIET
CALIFORNIA, USA

"And he said to her, 'Daughter, your faith has made you well. Go in peace. Your suffering is over.'"

—MARK 5:34 (NLT)

During the second semester of my freshman year of college I was diagnosed with adrenal fatigue. The symptoms came on gradually and then eventually took over my everyday life. What began as exhaustion turned into extreme fatigue with episodes of fainting and collapsing in bed for sometimes 20 hours at a time. I had to go to the emergency room multiple times before I was diagnosed with this condition. I spent most of my days lying in bed disoriented and extremely weak.

As my condition worsened, I began working with teachers to make up schoolwork because I was unable to attend classes and take tests. I considered taking a medical leave from college because my body could not keep up with the demands of school. Even after months of working with doctors and nutritionists, I did not get better. My mom decided to take me to a worship night at a local church. She had been praying earnestly for me to be healed and wanted me to be in the presence of God.

Friday night we attended a worship service with mostly young people and college age students. My mom and I sat on the floor in the back of the room as we joined in to worship God. After what felt like hours of worship, a group of girls started dancing and praising God. They laughed with joy and delight as they held hands in a circle, dancing and running throughout the room.

As I sat in the corner watching this, I felt envious, saying to myself, "I wish I could have the strength to even go for a walk let alone do anything as exciting as dance around a room having fun and praising God." I complained to the Lord as I felt the frustration of my own circumstance build. It had been months since I had even lived a normal day.

Then, after what felt like several minutes of self-pity, I heard a voice speak to me and say, "Get up, you're healed." I sat there for a few minutes wondering if I had just heard the voice of God. I did not feel healed, and I definitely did not feel any change to my condition. I had grown so weak over the last few months, that even getting up to stand was an activity in itself.

I sat there a few moments longer looking down at my shoe realizing I had a decision to make: I could either believe that

I had heard God and get up and trust that I was healed, or I could continue to sit there staring at the floor complaining to God about my condition. I decided to get up, and as I stood, I immediately felt my energy return. I began to run around the room joining the other girls dancing and praising God. I was instantly healed, and my energy was fully restored as though I had never been weak or sick at all.

As I started running and dancing around the room the pastor noticed what had happened. He asked me to share my testimony. I told everyone how God had instantly healed me. The pastor asked if anybody else in the room needed a miracle. A girl my age raised her hand and said she tore her ACL and did not want to have surgery on her knee. The pastor told me to go pray for her, so I, along with some others, went to her side to pray for her. After a few minutes of praying for her, nothing happened.

The people around us left to go back to where everyone was worshipping. I asked her to continue to pray with me as she laid there on the floor clutching her knee in pain. Still nothing happened and I became nervous because I did not know what to do. I asked her if she knew how to pray in tongues and she said "yes," and we began to pray in tongues together for what felt like another 15 minutes.

Again, nothing seemed to happen. So, then I said "OK, I am going to continue to pray in tongues and I want you to stop thinking about your knee and just pray in tongues and praise God." Then after what felt like one or two minutes, she jumped up and started dancing and kicking her knees out in different directions while praising God at the top of her lungs. I stood there amazed. We both started praising God and joined back into the worship celebration with singing and dancing and rejoicing and praising God.

From that night on I was completely healed and went back to my normal life at college. I was able to go back to classes, do school activities, and exercise as though I had never been sick at all. I was fully restored. It was truly a miracle! Praise the Lord!

Prayer: *Heavenly Father God, thank You for healing, restoring, and redeeming. You are a good God and an amazing Creator. Thank You for the gift of life. Amen!*

24.
ALL THINGS ARE POSSIBLE WITH GOD

BY TIM FORSTHOFF
MICHIGAN, USA

"But they who wait for the Lord shall renew their strength; they shall mount up with wings like eagles; they shall run and not be weary; they shall walk and not faint."

—ISAIAH 40:31 (ESV)

I would like to share an amazing testimony of God's amazing healing power. Approximately 15 years ago, I went to the doctor for my annual physical. He took a blood test and found my liver enzymes were elevated. He took more tests and confirmed the initial report. I had liver problems. I wasn't sure what that meant but I was sent to a liver specialist for consultation.

Upon running additional tests, the doctor sent me to Henry Ford Hospital in Detroit where I was diagnosed with cirrhosis of the liver. Cirrhosis of the liver is a chronic disease that is marked by degeneration of cells, inflammation, and thickening of tissue. It is a life-threatening disease. It is usually caused by hepatitis or alcoholism.

The doctor put me on a waiting list for a liver transplant. He told me to check every day for yellowing of my eyes and skin. He said I should contact him immediately if I saw any yellowing when I looked in the mirror. I was anxious and fearful. Every day I would check myself in the mirror. Every day I would ask Jesus to heal me.

During this very challenging time, I came down with a very bad cold. I was driving to work one morning and my heart started beating really fast. This continued for a few days, so I called my doctor. He listened to my heart and immediately sent me to a heart specialist. After a series of tests, the doctor told me I had a heart arrhythmia. The doctor told me that the virus attacked my heart and threw it into an arrhythmia. This is an irregular heartbeat. It felt like I had an active bee's nest in my chest. My heart would beat so fast that I couldn't sleep at night.

In addition, my heart was enlarged. An enlarged heart is a weakened heart. This went on for two years. I would see the liver doctor and the heart doctor. I would never receive a good report from either one of them. Every day I would pray for God to heal me.

God began to speak promises from His Word to me. Here are a few of them:

"You shall walk in all the ways which the Lord your God has commanded you, that you may live and that it may be well with you, and that you may prolong your days in the land which you shall possess."

—DEUTERONOMY 5:33 (NKJV)

"My heart is steadfast, O God, my heart is steadfast; I will sing and give praise."

—PSALMS 57:7 (NKJV)

God promised me long life, length of days, with a strong heart to praise the Lord.

After approximately two years of a liver issue, a heart arrhythmia, and an anxious mind, I woke up one morning and everything was changed. My chest was not buzzing like a bee hive. It was calm and felt normal. I went to my heart doctor who did a series of tests and found my heartbeat was normal. He also measured the size of my heart and that was also normal.

I then scheduled an appointment with my liver doctor who was surprised to find my liver enzymes had returned to normal. He would continue to test me every six months. After two additional years of testing, I was told I did not have to return for any more testing. My liver had returned to normal.

Listen to what the psalmist says, "Oh, give thanks to the LORD, for He is good! For His mercy endures forever. Let the redeemed of the LORD say so, Whom He has redeemed from the hand of the enemy" (Psalm 107:1-2 NKJV).

I learned to trust in God's love. God really does care for me. I learned to trust in God's power. All things are possible with God. And I learned to trust in God's timing. It is good to wait on the Lord.

Prayer: *Father God, all things are possible with You. Do the impossible in my life. Do miracles in me. Use me for Your glory. In Jesus' name, amen.*

25.
GOD HEALED MY VOICE

BY LORI HATCHER
TEXAS, USA

"Some men came carrying a paralyzed man on a sleeping mat. They tried to take him inside to Jesus, but they couldn't reach him because of the crowd. So they went up to the roof and took off some tiles. Then they lowered the sick man on his mat down into the crowd, right in front of Jesus."

—LUKE 5:18-19 (NLT)

My voice was shot. Basically, down to a raspy whisper. It was early summer of 1981. Our 36-member musical group, "Living Praise," just came off a whirlwind European tour. Right out of the gate we were launching our US state side summer tour. Our first stop was our home base, Christ for the Nations, in Dallas, Texas. We were refueling, repacking and set to serve and lead worship at a "revival weekend." The campus was filled to the brim with guests—buzzing with people who traveled near and far, expecting to receive a refreshing from the Lord.

One of the keynote speakers for the event was Evangelist Reinhard Bonnke. At this point in his ministry, Reinhard Bonnke spoke broken English. One thing he knew well to communicate was the power of Jesus Christ to heal and deliver. When he spoke the Word of God many were healed and changed. At each evening event the auditorium was packed.

As mentioned, our whole group was exhausted. Honestly, I just wanted to head to my dorm room for a few hours of rest. Then, my dear friend—one of my best friends—John Hatcher, urged me to go to the altar (front area of the room) to receive prayer for my lost voice. He was insistent, and I complied. Brother Reinhard was surrounded with people; however, his assistant was moving through the area where we stood (on the outskirts of the packed altar). He touched my head and said the name of Jesus. I felt nothing. Nonetheless, I believed in the supernatural power of prayer in Jesus' name.

I was raised to believe Jesus heals. Mom was very active in her faith and praying for others. Miracles were not uncommon. Dad also believed and professed strong faith. We were raised to believe Jesus was the same, yesterday, today and forever.

"Jesus Christ is the same yesterday, today, and forever."

—HEBREWS 13:8 (NKJV)

Three nights after this, I was standing and ministering on the platform of a large church in the Bible Belt area. Lip syncing was my new normal. Director Bob Mason directed me to not use my vocal cords so I didn't do further damage. As he continued to train us to minister, he reminded the whole group something like, "our main ministry in Living Praise is leading people into a deeper lifestyle of worshiping the Lord. He told the group Lori would be lip-syncing, ministering through worship and praise through my heart and countenance of joy unto the Lord." In other words, he did not "bench" me.

Our main task, while ministering in song—was asking the Spirit of the Lord to download who in attendance He was assigning each of us to pray for. My heart was set to receive His instructions. After the singing concluded, we were instructed to minister at the altar of each congregation, and even go and minister to the person or people the Lord had laid on our heart.

Again, three days after being prayed for at the altar, I was standing with the group and going through each song—singing in my heart but my voice uttered no sound. This particular evening, at the beginning of the concert, my friend John took to his mic and began to do something off script (the band and sound techs were all part of it), but Bob was not. John began introducing each band member as if he were performing at the Johnny Carson Tonight Show. "This evening, on the drums, all the way from Dallas, Texas, is the amazing Mike Wells; at the electric guitar, the incomparable, Tommy Walker from the Pacific Coast" and so on. Bob, the church and our group started having a moment of joy and fun.

Immediately, while laughing—my full voice returned. I was shocked and began to tear up. The moment segued into Bob speaking about the joy of the Lord. And he introduced our starting number. Our singers were positioned from the tallest on each side, descending to the shortest in the middle, where Bob stood in front leading. I was near Bob, as I was (and am) a bit short.

At the start of the song, I sang full voice, not saying anything to anyone about the change I was experiencing. Bob Mason was stunned. He privately said to me, "Lori, are you singing?!" "Bob, my voice is healed!" I replied.

Bob began to set up the next song. Without saying anything to the group, he quietly alerted a fellow student, who was filling in for my solo verse, that I would be singing the solo. My dear friend looked a bit confused, as all knew my voice was basically a whisper. As the time led up to the solo, I began to belt out the words in a clear, 100% capacity voice. Needless to say, the members of the group rejoiced—some cried tears of worship. It was a miracle witnessed by my friends.

The joy of the Lord, including this miracle, absolutely gave our fatigued group a boost of strength. I have experienced miracles in my life as a believer in Jesus. This particular miracle was quite impactful to my life. It was surrounded by joy. It was not based on my emotions. It was experienced by my friends and colleagues in Jesus. 40 years later, it's as if it were yesterday. I will never forget it.

John, who urged me to go to the altar, and who set up the moment of joy, soon became my amazing husband! John acted like one of the tenacious friends who pulled the roof apart to get their friend closer to Jesus (Luke 5:17-26). In our 40 plus years together (including four decades of ministry) we have experienced God's great faithfulness and miracle working power.

***Prayer:** Heavenly Father God, fill me with Your overwhelming joy today! Amen.*

26. GOD HEALED ME WHEN THE DOCTOR SAID I COULDN'T BE HEALED

BY NAOKO TAKAHASHI
TOKYO, JAPAN

"If you abide in me, and my words abide in you, ask whatever you wish, and it will be done for you."

—JOHN 15:7 (ESV)

I met Jesus when I was 15 years old while living in Bangkok, Thailand. I was raised in a family with many problems; it was an environment in which I could hardly find love and support. I became the only Christian in my family.

After graduating from university, my father introduced me to a Japanese trading company. I was assigned to the overseas sales team, a department where my colleagues worked until midnight and hard work was the norm.

Although I was bewildered by the Japanese company system, I worked hard every day because my father had introduced me to this company. However, a few months after joining the company, the knots in my body began to ache, and going to work every morning became a chore. It was hell to push through the fatigue and the pain in my body and ride the crowded train to work, taking almost two hours each way every day.

At that time, my parents were stationed in Chicago and my sisters and I were living alone in a house. My mother was abusive in our childhood and my sisters and I didn't get along with each other, so I had no place at home or at work. I spent many days battling physical pain. When I was feeling the limits of my health and work, I met my now husband at church.

When I met him, I felt relieved that I had finally found a friend with whom I could share my feelings. I felt that I didn't have to push myself anymore, and all the tension I had been holding back was suddenly lifted.

Around that time, my pain symptoms became worse day by day, and finally I had to crawl on the floor to go to the bathroom. I went to see many doctors, but none of them could give me a correct diagnosis.

One day, on my way home from work, I ran out of energy and collapsed; I laid down on a bench on the platform at the train station. I was in pain and too tired to go home.

Just then, a doctor and my former teacher from college walked by and was surprised to see me lying on the bench and listened to my story. Hearing my symptoms, he told me to go immediately to a large hospital for tests. I was 24 years old then.

I immediately went to a big hospital to be examined as the doctor told me to do. That hospital happened to have a specialist who was well known for the disease I had; I was diagnosed with fibromyalgia. It is a disease that drives you crazy with pain and fatigue.

No amount of painkillers will relieve the pain. There is no known cure to this day.

The cause of the disease is also unknown. As soon as I found out the name of the disease, I was at a loss as to what I was going to do at work and how I was going to explain this to my family.

The doctor told me that I would have to live with it for the rest of my life, as it would never be completely cured. By that time, I was bedridden and unable to take a single step.

I was immediately hospitalized and ended up staying in the hospital for six months. After trying various medications and suffering from side effects, I was eventually forced to live in a wheelchair, and after being discharged from the hospital, I went out in a wheelchair and could barely walk around the house.

There is no established treatment. The side effects of the medications are harsh. I was in pain and unable to move. I lived with the disease for eight years in my 20s and 30s.

During that time, God gave me a chance to get married to a wonderful man.

One day, I prayed to God. Please release me from the pain. Please heal me from this disease. I had asked God many times for my illness to go away. However, I remember that at that time, I asked clearly.

Sometime later, my mother-in-law told me that a pastor with a gift of healing was coming from the U.S. and that there would be a meeting. My husband took me, although I was in a wheelchair when I left the house and used a cane when I walked a little.

At the meeting, I was told that anyone who wanted to be healed should come forward, and I went to the pastor with the sole intention of being healed.

Then that pastor looked at me and immediately said, now, Jesus touched your body there and healed you, you are healed, drop the cane and run in a big circle around this hall. He said to me, "You are healed."

My mind went, "What is he talking about, running?" At the same time, I was convinced that yes, the Lord had healed me.

And for the first time in eight years, I ran; I did a big loop around that venue! I was so surprised and filled with joy. But perhaps who was even more surprised was my husband!

After I got healed, I went to see my doctor. I'll never be able to express the look on his face as I walked in the door without the cane and wheelchair! He almost fell from the chair.

"What?! You're healed?! That's unbelievable, but I'm so happy for you!!" The test results I took turned out to be normal and the doctors were really surprised.

I then took up running and even ran a half marathon. I also resumed travel, sports, and my favorite hobby, piano, which I had not been able to compete in for many years.

Later on, my terrible allergies were healed, and when I had polyps on my body, they disappeared when I trusted God and gave thanks to Him.

I know that there is nothing that God cannot do. When you truly ask God, your Creator, to do something, He hears you. God hears. He also teaches me a lesson at the same time.

When something goes wrong, don't take the problem around with you and go elsewhere. I remind myself to turn to God alone, keep my eyes on God alone, and just thank and praise Him.

We all have hills and valleys in our lives. I will make note to remember this lesson and turn to God no matter what. I believe that is what we are called for until we meet Jesus in eternity. May glory be to the name of Jesus alone.

Prayer: *Thank You Father God, You can do all things! There's nothing too difficult for You! Help me trust You more and more every day! Do a miracle in my life today. I love You! In Jesus' name I pray, amen.*

27.
THE DEAF HEAR

BY VERENA LIMA
PARÁ, BRAZIL

"Don't worry about anything; instead, pray about everything. Tell God what you need, and thank him for all he has done."

—PHILIPPIANS 4:6 (NLT)

Ivoneide came to our clinic asking if we had a specific doctor to treat her ear. Unfortunately, we did not.

Two years prior, she had experienced a strong headache and a very loud noise in her ears. After that experience, she lost 100% of the hearing in her left ear. The only thing we could do for her was pray. We prayed three times until Jesus worked a miracle in this woman's life.

She could not even express the joy she was feeling. She did not know Jesus so we preached the gospel to her and immediately she made a decision for Jesus.

It is beautiful to see how miracles open doors to salvation. We are thankful to God to be a part of these experiences. Oftentimes, especially in our limitations, we can how our God is truly great!

Prayer: *Heavenly Father God, thank You for doing miracles and opening up people's hearts to You. Increase my faith and help me to expect miracles when I pray. Help me to trust You more and believe You to do what only You can do! In Jesus' Name, amen.*

28.
GOD HEALED MY DAD

BY LORI BUNK
MICHIGAN, USA

"And Jesus answered them, "Have faith in God. Truly, I say to you, whoever says to this mountain, 'Be taken up and thrown into the sea,' and does not doubt in his heart, but believes that what he says will come to pass, it will be done for him. Therefore I tell you, whatever you ask in prayer, believe that you have received it, and it will be yours."

—MARK 11:22-24 (ESV)

On April 7, 2021, I received a phone call that my dad stopped breathing and was in transit to the hospital by ambulance. I sent a 911 text to my sister and she raced from work to beat his ambulance to the Emergency Room to meet my mom and her husband who were following. The cardiologist was already there and we were told my dad had a cardiac arrest because of a 100% blockage in his left anterior descending artery, also known as the "widow maker."

My dad never woke up that day.

In fact, day after day, my dad remained in the Intensive Care Unit (ICU) on a ventilator with no response. None of us were allowed to walk into the hospital because of the restrictions brought by the world-wide pandemic, so ICU nurses would graciously make their personal phones available for us to FaceTime for 5-10 minutes a day.

But there was no one there to sit at his bedside. No one to hold his hand. No one to pray into his ear for the Lord to restore life in his body or recite scriptures of God's promise to heal. We held on to the truth that God was present in his hospital room and working on his behalf, whether we could see it with our own eyes or not.

The hospital staff did their best to exhaust every resource at their disposal, but on the 6th day we were told we needed to start preparing ourselves for the difficult conversation of taking him off the ventilator permanently. We understood that even if they were able to keep him alive, his brain most likely had suffered irreversible damage.

My mom's faith was never shaken. She was steadfast in her confidence that God was not finished working His good through my dad. Our family (mom, me and my siblings, and 13 grandkids) stood unrelenting in prayer day after day. People were gathering all over the world to pray for my dad in areas my parents traveled for mission work and our home church had a standing early morning prayer meeting to cry out to God on my dad's behalf. The prognosis was clear. We knew the statistics. We heard what the medical community was telling us was true, and that he was given less than a 1% chance to live. But we also knew our God. We chose to stand unapologetically on His truth and promise.

On the 8th day, my brother-in-law, Tommy, was in the hospital parking lot praying and felt impressed by God to go in, knowing we had been told extensively that would never be a viable option. God made a way, and he was able to FaceTime us from my father's ICU room. As Tommy laid hands on him for the 1st time, our family began to pray over him. My dad began to respond with a big yawn and opened his eyes, looking at each of us with tears running down his face. We were confident something had shifted.

On day 10, they took my dad off the ventilator and he could freely breathe on his own. Each day he gained back the ability to move, speak, and walk and was released from the hospital just a few days later. There was a recovery road he was obliged to walk, but with every passing day, God worked abundant healing in my dad's body and mind. He is a living miracle of the power of God to heal and restore life to that which was marked for death.

Prayer: *Heavenly Father God, thank You for Your marvelous grace and healing power. Increase my faith. Help me to not waver in the midst of crisis but to trust You. In Jesus' name I pray, amen.*

EMOTIONAL HEALINGS

29.
MY SHATTERED HEART IS BEING MADE WHOLE AGAIN

BY DEBBIE BLOCK
KANAGAWA, JAPAN

"He heals the brokenhearted and bandages their wounds."

—PSALM 147:3 (NLT)

I looked over at my husband holding our lifeless newborn daughter and with tears pouring out of my eyes I said through the sobs, "I have a broken heart."

I never knew what a broken heart felt like before. I grew up in a very loving, Christian home as a missionary kid in Brazil. Though I was a little blonde girl living in a dangerous city in the Amazon Basin, nothing significantly bad ever happened to me. When I was 17, I moved to the United States to go to college. I went to a Christian university, had lots of friends, was on the dance team, was in college leadership roles, double majored with great grades, and to top it off, I married my college sweetheart. My husband Ben is a pastor and I served alongside him at an amazing church in Michigan for almost seven years. During that time, we had our first two beautiful daughters right in the timeframe we were hoping for.

In 2019, we moved to Japan as missionaries, continuing to serve the Lord with all our hearts and lives. Adjusting to the new culture, new language, and new lifestyle was challenging, but we enjoyed the new adventure and we were obeying God's calling on our lives. I got pregnant with our third daughter Eliana, and that pregnancy felt like "the hardest time in my life." The pregnancy itself was fine, but having a growing family in Tokyo where I still was not fluent in the language was very hard for me. However, it was nothing compared to what was to come.

Before Eliana turned one, we found out I was pregnant with our fourth daughter! While not planned, we were excited that the Lord was granting the desires of our hearts to have four children (and back-to-back!). I promptly started planning, dreaming, envisioning what life would be like upon the arrival of our last child, the completion of our family unit.

Everything about the pregnancy was smooth until the middle of my third trimester. That's when the itching began. This was something I was familiar with because I had been diagnosed with Intrahepatic Cholestasis of Pregnancy (ICP) during my second pregnancy, and the main symptom is itching. But with that pregnancy in the U.S., my doctor was able to diagnose the condition, treat it, and praise God, deliver a healthy baby. This time around, that was not the case. The condition was only detected after it was too late.

Two weeks before my due date, I stopped feeling our baby move inside of me and we started living a nightmare. Ben took me to the hospital, and the silence of the doppler and ultrasound were deafening. Where there was once a strong heart beating, there was only a black void. Our sweet Esther Joelle was in heaven with Jesus. I delivered her via c-section on September 16, 2021. We had prayer warriors on a zoom call that lasted longer than 36 hours. We held our baby girl and prayed, and prayed, and prayed over her. We longed to see the beautiful miracle of Jesus' resurrection power displayed in our little daughter, but that was not the miracle we saw.

The miracle that we did see and are experiencing daily as life goes on is the healing of broken hearts, the comfort of the Holy Spirit, and the hope we have anchored in our souls. This loss completely devastated me. I didn't know how I would be able to get out of bed each morning. How would I be able to be the mom that my living girls needed me to be and the wife my husband needed me to be? I didn't know if my smile would ever be genuine again. How can a person so broken by the tragedy of loss continue living with joy and hope? I have discovered that it is through the mercy of the Lord, the miraculous power of God.

Psalm 30:10-12 (NLT) says, "Hear me, LORD, and have mercy on me. Help me, O Lord. You have turned my mourning into joyful dancing. You have taken away my clothes of mourning and clothed me with joy, that I might sing praises to you and not be silent. O LORD my God, I will give you thanks forever!"

The day Ben picked up the urn with our daughter's ashes inside, I highlighted these verses in my Bible:

"To all who mourn in Israel, he will give a crown of beauty for ashes, a joyous blessing instead of mourning, festive praise instead of despair."

—ISAIAH 61:3 (NLT)

"Great is his faithfulness; his mercies begin afresh each morning. I say to myself, 'The LORD is my inheritance; therefore, I will hope in him!'"

—LAMENTATIONS 3:23-24 (NLT)

Instead of abandoning my faith in the One who could have resurrected our baby girl but did not, I chose to cling on to Jesus with all that I had left. I made a conscious choice to believe Isaiah 55:8-9 (NLT). It says, "'My thoughts are nothing like your thoughts,' says the LORD. 'And my ways are far beyond anything you could imagine. For just as the heavens are higher than the earth, so my ways are higher than your ways and my thoughts higher than your thoughts.'"

In doing so, I am experiencing what I thought was impossible: my shattered heart is being made whole again. The Bible is a source of life, filled with cries of pain and agony, then followed by the reassurance that God's love and compassion for us is far greater than we can ever comprehend but can experience on a daily basis. I'm living proof that "The LORD is close to the brokenhearted; he rescues those whose spirits are crushed" (Psalm 34:18 NLT).

"Unless the LORD had helped me, I would soon have settled in the silence of the grave. I cried out, 'I am slipping!' but your unfailing love, O LORD, supported me. When doubts filled my mind, your comfort gave me renewed hope and cheer."

—PSALM 94:17-19 (NLT)

"He lifted me out of the pit of despair, out of the mud and the mire. He set my feet on solid ground and steadied me as I walked along. He has given me a new song to sing, a hymn of praise to our God. Many will see what he has done and be amazed. They will put their trust in the LORD."

—PSALM 40:2-3 (NLT)

That last verse is my prayer moving forward. I pray that many will see what the Lord has done in lifting me out of the depression I had quickly slipped into after my loss; I pray many will see the healing of my broken heart, and how God has put a new song in my mouth, and is giving me true joy and hope as I continue to live; and I pray that they will put their trust in our awesome God.

"I pray that God, the source of hope, will fill you completely with joy and peace because you trust in him. Then you will overflow with confident hope through the power of the Holy Spirit."

—ROMANS 15:13 (NLT)

Prayer: *Father God, heal my heart. Restore my soul. Make me whole. Give me joy and peace and hope. In Jesus' name I pray, amen.*

30.
GOD IS FAITHFUL TO REDEEM

BY NICOLE KALOWICK
MICHIGAN, USA

"'But I will restore you to health and heal your wounds,' declares the Lord."

—JEREMIAH 30:17 (NIV)

Before I even knew of the words *trauma* or *grief*, I had experienced the reality of them in my life. I couldn't have told you the definition or how to process through them, but as a young child, I knew what they were and how they felt.

When I was three years old my mom was diagnosed with a terminal cancer. The tumor formed at the base of her neck and wrapped around her spinal cord. The prognosis was bleak. Surgery couldn't be done and chemo had very little effect. The doctors basically sought to "keep her comfortable till the end."

I am thankful to have come from a strong family of believers. The moment the prognosis came in, my family stood on the Word of God and fought on my mother's behalf. And, honestly, on mine.

"The Lord sustains them on their sickbed and restores them from their bed of illness."

—PSALM 41:3 (NIV)

"Is anyone among you sick? Let them call the elders of the church to pray over them and anoint them with oil in the name of the Lord."

—JAMES 5:14 (NIV)

They prayed, fasted, spoke the Word, brought my mom to church gatherings to be prayed for and believed in her healing whole heartedly. (So much so in fact that her doctors and nurses were concerned. Her medical papers read in a few locations "patient, not fully aware or willing to accept prognosis").

During this time however my mom was slowly and strategically being coerced by a supposed "Christian" leader of a healing-centered ministry. Over time this man manipulated, gaslighted, and deceived my mom into believing many lies.

The process took months and months, but eventually the coercion led to my mom trying to divorce my dad, my families bank account information being taken, and eventually leading to my brother, myself and my mom being abducted.

The abduction was a slow process. It started off with just a few weekends away to be a part of the alleged "ministry" and over time turned into a few weeks, then months away with limited contact.

For a period of time, me and my brother only saw my family, including my father, for a few short visits near Christmas (hard time of the year for a predator to find an excuse for family not to visit with their children and grandchildren). These moments allowed my family to still have connection to us and get a pulse on what was actually occurring.

I honestly can only recall a few pieces of memory from this time. My strongest memory is being locked in a large play room filled with toys and feeling so uncomfortable with the couple that was assigned to take care of me and my brother. I remember feeling confused and scared; however, I knew it wasn't okay or potentially safe for me to express that to anyone.

In my mind's eye I can still see the demented, dark, and sinister faces of the two people who took care of us. I know they were normal people and their physical faces were not sinister or naturally evil looking, but that's what I saw. They were warped, dark, and evil. It's an image that is ingrained in my memory to this day.

I later learned that while me and my brother were left to play. My mom was locked in another room, drugged and emotionally and sexually abused. My family has never fully disclosed to me the details of what my mom experienced, but I've been told "that man was an evil, disgusting, and vial human." If I endured any comparable abuse during this time, I could not tell you.

Back in the early 90's, when this was occurring, people didn't know about "trafficking", "coercion" or anything regarding situations like these. It was not talked about and no one knew what "signs" to look for or even what trafficking really was. Therefore, no one believed my grandparents when they shared that something was wrong.

My grandparents knew their daughter, they knew the Lord, and knew that they would not sit idly by and watch their family dissipate. So, they didn't! They prayed, fought, and as my grandma often says "we became like the persistent widow in the Bible" (see Luke 18:1-8 NIV).

My grandparents did not relent and tried and tried, over and over again to break through the veil the ministry leaders were blind to. The ministry did not know or even have a glimpse into the evil behind the man they allowed to lead on their team. This battle went on for months.

Finally, my grandmother wrote a personal letter to the wife of the head ministry leader and mailed it to her home address to ensure it would get to her. My grandmother pleaded with her to "return my family". The wife had no prior knowledge of my family's connection with this man and no insight into our previous attempts made in sharing the truth to the deceived ministry leadership. The letter hit her to her core.

My family had been ignored, mocked and turned away numerous times. But now, a personal note from a pleading grandmother to another grandmother caused a powerful rippling effect. This man was ordered to cease any and all contact with my family and we were returned home.

It wasn't until years later that the ministry became fully aware of this man's evil doings.

"And will not God bring about justice for his chosen ones, who cry out to him day and night? Will he keep putting them off? I tell you, he will see that they get justice, and quickly. However, when the Son of Man comes, will he find faith on the earth?"

—LUKE 18:7-8 (NIV)

After returning home, my mom quickly lost mobility from the neck down. Her body was weak and failing her. She was also mentally deeply wounded and battling a spiritual and emotional attack.

My grandparents both retired from work and spent the remainder of my mother's life (about three months) taking care of her physically and helping the Lord bring healing back to her mentally and spiritually. They read scripture to her day and night. Prayed over her and before she passed away, the Lord brought restoration to her mind and spirit. I was only five years old when my mom passed away.

So much of the story I shared above has been navigated and made clearer to me through time. To this day (as a 30-year-old woman) I still get pieces of the story or memories that come back. I deal with very real trauma responses and triggers. I can get hit with an overwhelming feeling of fear, loss, and grief that is suffocating. One true thing remains though, God is faithful.

"You intended to harm me, but God intended it for good to accomplish what is now being done, the saving of many lives."

—GENESIS 50:20 (NIV)

The devil intended great evil for me and my family. He might have taken my mother's life here on earth but God was faithful in redeeming her mind and spirit. She is rejoicing in heaven—whole, complete and without pain. The devil might have wanted to entrap me in slavery, but everyday my God brings comfort to my pain and healing to my heart. He walks with me through every dark hour and every overwhelming moment.

"'For I know the plans I have for you,' declares the Lord, 'plans to prosper you and not to harm you, plans to give you hope and a future.'"

—JEREMIAH 29:11 (NIV)

I don't know your life, your past or even your present. I don't know if you have heavy and very real trauma like me or if you have walked through life's ups and down with ease. But I know the God who does know. He is the same God that saved my life over and over again. The same God that used my persistent grandmother to compel a heart that led to my freedom. The same God who treasured my mom enough to restore her mentally and spiritually before she left us. The same God who has carried me through every panic attack, nightmare, depression, insecurity, fear, hopelessness, loss and grief-filled moments and into a life of healing, purpose, joy and redemption.

My life is far from perfect but it is a life seeking to be close to the One who is. Close to the God who is faithful to redeem.

Prayer: *Heavenly Father God, thank You for renewing my mind. Help me sleep in peace at night trusting You and knowing You are God and in control. In Jesus' name, amen.*

31.
JESUS KNOWS WHAT I'M GOING THROUGH

BY BAILEY KUERT
OKLAHOMA, USA

"He gives power to the weak and strength to the powerless. Even youths will become weak and tired, and young men will fall in exhaustion. But those who trust in the Lord will find new strength. They will soar high on wings like eagles. They will run and not grow weary. They will walk and not faint."

—ISAIAH 40:29-31 (NLT)

I was raised very closely with my cousin, Tess who was four months older than I was. We were basically raised as sisters because our moms were each other's only sisters and we lived in the same city. Our moms even kept us together on weekdays until elementary school, assuring we'd be close.

We had a special bond and as we got older, we'd figure out a way to spend most weekends together.

When we were seven years old, Tess was unfortunately diagnosed with kidney cancer. My world seemed to spin in slow motion over the following seven years as I watched Tess battle cancer. She went through various treatments and surgeries, she went into remission, relapsed a couple of times, and continuously suffered. Sadly, when we were both in the first semester of our freshman year of High School, Tess passed away.

The pain I experienced in my heart was unlike anything I had experienced before. At the time, I didn't know where to turn. I knew about the things of God and I would've said that I was a Christian. However, I didn't attend church, and it wasn't until I heard a pastor a couple of years after her death talk about having a relationship with Jesus that salvation officially made sense to me. I had lost my very best friend and there was a void in my heart that no other relationship could fulfill until that day.

Over the coming weeks, months, and years, as I continued to grow in my relationship with Jesus, I realized that He not only saved me, but He met me in my grief and in other painful experiences.

When I was newly married, the anniversary of Tess' death came around again and that particular day brought a fresh and large wave of grief over me. I wept that morning and I felt so lonely. While I knew that Jesus cared, I felt like He couldn't actually relate to my sorrow and I even felt shame that I was still experiencing such grief.

I prayed that Jesus would once again meet me in my pain and help me. That same day, I had a conversation with my husband who reminded me that Jesus did in fact know what it felt like to lose His cousin. He would've known a close-in-age relationship with His cousin too, John the Baptist.

As I sat there meditating on how Jesus knew the same pain I was carrying, it made the price he paid to carry my sins and sorrows so much more tangibly real. It moved from head knowledge to tangibly knowing that He really can identify with my grief because he has felt the crushing weight of it. There began once again a deep work of healing that came to me not only for this area of suffering I carried, but in other areas as well. When I knew that Jesus was deeply acquainted with grief and that He could relate to my own loss, all of a sudden, I didn't feel alone in my pain.

I've had the great joy of seeing miracles of Jesus around the world. I've seen healing miracles, I've seen people set free from addictions, and I've seen His Spirit moving in incredibly dark places. All of that humbles me and makes me in awe of Christ's power and love, but I never want to overlook the miracle of Him being near to me in my sorrows, of Him relating to me as one who walked through what I walk through. While it may seem like a simple miracle to some, I am grateful to serve a Savior who is powerful enough to heal the blind and also humble enough to sit with me in my tears.

Prayer: *Heavenly Father, please meet me where I am at today. Please comfort me and heal my heart. Thank You for seeing me and walking through difficult times with me. Your grace is sufficient for me. In Jesus' name I pray, amen.*

CONCLUSION

Wow, I loved reading these stories! The Bible says that "God shows no partiality" (Acts 10:11 NKJV). You can pray and see mountains moved. You can ask God your Father for miracles and He can do the impossible.

I truly believe God's word is for us still today:

"And the prayer of faith will save the sick, and the Lord will raise him up. And if he has committed sins, he will be forgiven. Confess your trespasses to one another, and pray for one another, that you may be healed. The effective, fervent prayer of a righteous man avails much. Elijah was a man with a nature like ours, and he prayed earnestly that it would not rain; and it did not rain on the land for three years and six months. And he prayed again, and the heaven gave rain, and the earth produced its fruit."

—JAMES 5:15-18 (NKJV)

Let's continue to pray, expect miracles, and look to our Heavenly Father who wants to be actively involved in our lives.

I pray this book has inspired you to believe God for your own miracles! You need them and the world needs them too!

May we see many more testimonies!

RECEIVE JESUS INTO YOUR LIFE

You can have a relationship with Jesus today. The Bible says:

"If you declare with your mouth, 'Jesus is Lord,' and believe in your heart that God raised him from the dead, you will be saved. For it is with your heart that you believe and are justified, and it is with your mouth that you profess your faith and are saved."

—ROMANS 10:9-10 (NIV)

Would you pray this prayer today and make Jesus the Lord and Savior of your life?

Heavenly Father, thank you for your Son, Jesus Christ. I believe He is Lord. I believe that Jesus died for my sins and rose again. Please forgive me of my sins. Give me a new life today. Fill me with Your Holy Spirit and help me live for You. In Jesus' name I pray, amen.

If you prayed that prayer from your heart the Bible says you became a new creation (2 Corinthians 5:17). It's now time for you to continue to grow in your relationship with Jesus. Start talking with God in prayer, read the Bible which is His word for us, and get plugged in to a Bible believing church. Your best life is right in front of you!

Please feel free to share with me as well. I'd love to celebrate your new life in Jesus! You can email me at ben.block@pazchurch.com and let me know of your decision to follow Jesus, or even your recommitment to Christ!

JOURNAL SECTION—
WRITE YOUR STORY

I want to give you some time and space to think about how God has moved in your own life.

Maybe you have had a dramatic conversion from your old life to following Jesus. Or perhaps your story is that God has reconciled your marriage or healed you in some way or provided for you when you needed it.

Whatever it is, I encourage you to take five minutes and think about the amazing things God has done and write them down.

This is your personal story that you can share with anyone at any time and give glory to God.

I encourage you to write it out and share it with at least one person this week!

1 Peter 3:15 (NIV) says: "But in your hearts revere Christ as Lord. Always be prepared to give an answer to everyone who asks you to give the reason for the hope that you have. But do this with gentleness and respect."

My personal story of what God has done in my life:

PLEASE SHARE THIS BOOK

If this book has been a blessing to you (I hope it has!) please share it with a friend and leave a review on Amazon. I'd love for this book to be a tool that encourages people in their faith in Jesus and inspires many to believe God for more amazing miraculous stories!

PLEASE SHARE YOUR STORY

It's in my heart to make more books like this one. If you would like to share your story of what God has done in your life please write it out in about one page and submit it to me by email at ben.block@pazchurch.com.

ABOUT PAZ INTERNATIONAL

Beginning first in the Amazon Basin, and then expanding throughout almost all 26 states of Brazil and into 6 additional countries, PAZ International represents a powerful movement in church-planting and disciple-making.

PAZ International envisions a world where thriving nationally-led churches proclaim the gospel of Christ to every person. To find out more information or to partner with this ministry go to pazinternational.org.

ABOUT MY JOURNEY TO JAPAN

"Are you willing?" God asked me.

"Yes," I replied.

"Then go," God answered.

God was speaking to me about the nations, asking if I was willing to go. I was 24 years old at that time. I had just gotten back from a seven-week missions trip to Thailand and still jet-lagging from the international trip home. I had been worshiping God with my acoustic guitar outside on my apartment deck around 1:00 in the morning. God's words not only interrupted my worship time, *they changed my life*.

The following year I was considering whether or not I should go on another missions trip. It would be a big commitment. But I had a word from God, "Then go." So I went, this time to India. Our team worked with many Indian children and their lives were touched in a powerful way—as was mine.

A little while after my trip to India, I was hired by Cornerstone Church and moved to Michigan. I went on several more missions trips while on staff there to places like Jamaica, Honduras, Nicaragua, and the Dominican Republic. One night at a young adults conference that our church hosted, I encountered God again. I went to the altar at the end of the message and surrendered to God the fact that I didn't feel like I had a big vision for my life. The Lord spoke to me, "The vision has already been given." And at that moment the vision of Paz International came to mind. They have a vision of planting 100,000 churches.

So I had a calling to the nations. I now had a calling to join Paz International and plant churches. But where was I supposed to go? Around that time Paz International was sending a large team of people to São Paulo, Brazil, and I wanted to be a part of it. However, God had other plans. Through prayer and confirmation of our leadership my wife and I felt God's leading to come to Japan.

Towards the end of 2018, we packed up our belongings, sold our home, and said goodbye to family and friends. With our two young daughters we moved to Japan in January of 2019 and quickly jumped into language studies and the ministry here. It's been an exciting journey! We're seeing God touch lives and save souls. Just recently our church prayed over a team of almost 50 people who are being sent out to plant another Paz Church here in Japan!

People have said Japan is a missionary graveyard. Well, not today. Not for us. And I pray it never will be again. God is moving and we believe the wave of revival is coming to Japan. We're so thankful God called us to be a part of it!

I invite you to join us on this journey. You can stay connected with me and my family as well as sign up for our email updates at theblockfam.com.

—Ben Block

Printed in Great Britain
by Amazon

48797624R00106